Language in use

PRE-INTERMEDIATE

Self-Study Workbook
with answer key

ADRIAN DOFF & CHRISTOPHER JONES

CAMBRIDGE
UNIVERSITY PRESS

PUBLISHED BY THE PRESS SYNDICATE OF THE UNIVERSITY OF CAMBRIDGE
The Pitt Building, Trumpington Street, Cambridge CB2 1RP, United Kingdom

CAMBRIDGE UNIVERSITY PRESS
The Edinburgh Building, Cambridge CB2 2RU, United Kingdom
40 West 20th Street, New York, NY 10011–4211, USA
10 Stamford Road, Oakleigh, Melbourne 3166, Australia

© Cambridge University Press 1991

First published 1991
Fifth printing 1997

Printed in the United Kingdom at the University Press, Cambridge

ISBN 0 521 40602 1 Self-study Workbook with Answer Key
ISBN 0 521 37852 4 Self-study Workbook
ISBN 0 521 37851 6 Classroom Book
ISBN 0 521 37853 2 Teacher's Book
ISBN 0 521 37248 8 Class Cassette Set
ISBN 0 521 37247 X Self-study Cassette Set
ISBN 0 521 55602 3 Tests
ISBN 0 521 55601 5 Tests Cassette

Split editions:
ISBN 0 521 40837 7 Self-study Workbook A with Answer Key
ISBN 0 521 40838 5 Self-study Workbook B with Answer Key
ISBN 0 521 40835 0 Classroom Book A
ISBN 0 521 40836 9 Classroom Book B
ISBN 0 521 40839 3 Self-study Cassette A
ISBN 0 521 40840 7 Self-study Cassette B

Contents

To the student

This Workbook contains exercises for you to do on your own.

Each Workbook unit begins with grammar or vocabulary exercises, which give extra practice in the language you have learned in class.

In addition, there are self-study exercises which help you to develop particular skills in English. These are:
- Listening skills (in each unit)
- Reading skills (in each Grammar unit)
- Writing skills (in each Topic unit)
- Pronunciation (in Grammar units) and Sound and spelling (in Topic units)

There are also two Self-study Cassettes that go with the Workbook. You will need to use these for the Listening, Pronunciation, Sound and spelling, and Dictation exercises.

Answers to most of the exercises are given in the Answer key at the back of the book.

Here is a short description of the exercises in the Workbook:

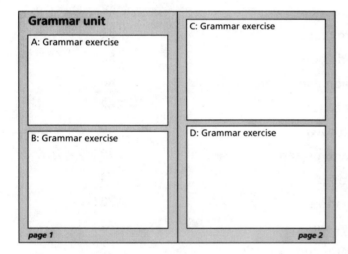

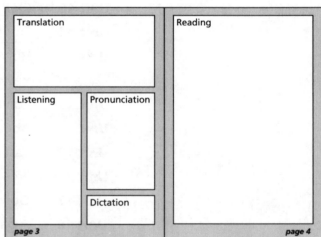

Grammar exercises
The grammar exercises give practice in the main structures of the unit. They usually include one puzzle or word game, and sometimes one freer exercise. There are three or four grammar exercises in each unit.

Translation
This section contains sentences for you to translate into your own language – and then back into English.

Listening
These are short listening tasks, which give you a chance to listen to natural English in your own time. Usually, the speakers are doing one of the activities from the Classroom Book.

Pronunciation
These exercises give practice in pronunciation, stress and intonation.

Dictation
You hear a short text taken from one of the Classroom Book exercises, and write it down.

Reading
This section contains reading tasks based on a variety of short texts. These include magazine and newspaper articles, personal letters, jokes, quizzes and stories.

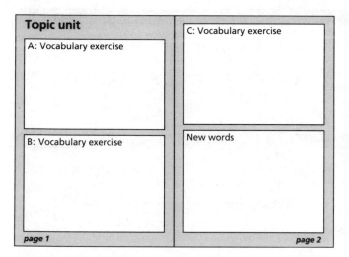

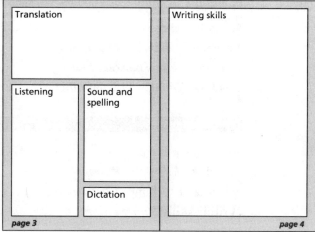

Vocabulary exercises

The vocabulary exercises give practice in the main vocabulary areas of the unit. They usually include one puzzle or word game, and sometimes one freer exercise. There are two or three vocabulary exercises in each unit.

New words

This is a space for you to write down new words from the unit, together with your own notes and examples.

Translation

This section contains sentences for you to translate into your own language – and then back into English.

Listening

These are short listening tasks, which give you a chance to listen to natural English in your own time. Usually, the speakers are doing one of the activities from the Classroom Book.

Sound and spelling

This section deals with the relationship between sound and spelling in English.

Dictation

You hear a short text taken from one of the Classroom Book exercises, and write it down.

Writing skills

These exercises teach the basic writing skills you need to write a paragraph in English. These include punctuation, using pronouns, joining sentences and organising ideas.

Guide to units

Self-study Workbook	Classroom Book
1 Description	
Grammar exercises Listening: *Asking for help* Pronunciation: *Where's the stress?* Reading: *Islands*	Saying what there is and where things are; describing features **Grammar:** There is/are; have/has got; place prepositions
2 Family and friends	
Vocabulary exercises Listening: *Relatives* Sound and spelling: *Words with* a Writing skills: *Sentences*	**Vocabulary:** family; relationships; love and marriage **Reading and listening activity:** *Are you a loner?*
3 Habits, customs and facts	
Grammar exercises Listening: *Japanese New Year* Pronunciation: *The sound /ə/* Reading: *Reptiles and amphibians*	Talking about repeated activities and things that are generally true **Grammar:** Present simple tense; frequency expressions
4 Going places	
Vocabulary exercises Listening: *Likes and dislikes* Sound and spelling: *Words with* e Writing skills: *Punctuation*	**Vocabulary:** vehicles; public transport; talking about travel **Reading and listening activity:** *Airport*
5 Now	
Grammar exercises Listening: *These days* Pronunciation: *Reduced vowels (1)* Reading: *What's going on?*	Talking about things happening 'now' and 'around now'; describing scenes **Grammar:** Present continuous tense; There is/are + -ing
6 Food and drink	
Vocabulary exercises Listening: *Polish dishes* Sound and spelling: *Words with* i Writing skills: *Reference*	**Vocabulary:** food and drink; meals; restaurants **Reading and listening activity:** *Cholesterol and your heart*
Revision and extension Units 1–6	

<table>
<tr><td>

Self-study Workbook

</td><td>

Classroom Book

</td></tr>
<tr><td colspan="2">

7 The past

</td></tr>
<tr><td>

Grammar exercises
Listening: *When did you last ... ?*
Pronunciation: *Reduced vowels (2)*
Reading: *Jokes*

</td><td>

Talking about past events; saying when things happened; telling stories
Grammar: Past simple tense; time expressions

</td></tr>
<tr><td colspan="2">

8 Somewhere to live

</td></tr>
<tr><td>

Vocabulary exercises
Listening: *Favourite rooms*
Sound and spelling: *Words with* o *(1)*
Writing skills: *Joining ideas*

</td><td>

Vocabulary: houses and flats; rooms and furniture
Reading and listening activity: *Haunted houses*

</td></tr>
<tr><td colspan="2">

9 Quantity

</td></tr>
<tr><td>

Grammar exercises
Listening: *Panel discussion*
Pronunciation: *Secondary stress*
Reading: *Money*

</td><td>

Talking about quantity; saying there is too much and not enough
Grammar: a/some/any; quantity expressions; How much/many ... ?; too & not enough

</td></tr>
<tr><td colspan="2">

10 Clothes

</td></tr>
<tr><td>

Vocabulary exercises
Listening: *Working clothes*
Sound and spelling: *Words with* o *(2)*
Writing skills: *Sequence (1)*

</td><td>

Vocabulary: items of clothing; materials and patterns; buying and wearing clothes
Reading and listening activity: *Going for gold*

</td></tr>
<tr><td colspan="2">

11 Future plans

</td></tr>
<tr><td>

Grammar exercises
Listening: *Two journeys*
Pronunciation: *Rhythm*
Reading: *Letters*

</td><td>

Talking about intentions and plans; talking about future arrangements
Grammar: going to; Present continuous tense; will; future time expressions

</td></tr>
<tr><td colspan="2">

12 How do you feel?

</td></tr>
<tr><td>

Vocabulary exercises
Listening: *Feeling ill*
Sound and spelling: *Words with* u
Writing skills: *Listing*

</td><td>

Vocabulary: aches and pains; remedies; going to the doctor
Reading and listening activity: *All in the mind*

</td></tr>
</table>

Revision and extension Units 7–12

Self-study Workbook	Classroom Book
13 Comparison	
Grammar exercises Listening: *The most and the least* Pronunciation: *Reduced vowels (3)* Reading: *Four planets*	Making comparisons; expressing preferences;describing outstanding features **Grammar:** comparative adjectives; than; superlative adjectives
14 About town	
Vocabulary exercises Listening: *Living in London* Sound and spelling: *Words with* y Writing skills: *Reason and contrast*	**Vocabulary:** amenities; giving directions; describing towns in general **Reading and listening activity:** *Los Angeles*
15 Past and present	
Grammar exercises Listening: *Have you ever … ?* Pronunciation: *Falling intonation* Reading: *Varieties of English*	Talking about changes; announcing news; talking about experiences **Grammar:** Present perfect tense; still; not … yet; Have you ever … ?
16 Free time	
Vocabulary exercises Listening: *Rock climbing* Sound and spelling: *Words with* r Writing skills: *Sequence (2)*	**Vocabulary:** leisure activities; sports; likes and dislikes **Reading and listening activity:** *Board games round the world*
17 Obligation	
Grammar exercises Listening: *Radio phone-in* Pronunciation: *Rising intonation* Reading: *Rules of the game*	Giving rules; talking about obligation; giving advice **Grammar:** must(n't); (don't) have to; can('t); should(n't); ought (not) to
18 A day's work	
Vocabulary exercises Listening: *A security guard* Sound and spelling: *Hard and soft* c *and* g Writing skills: *Letter writing*	**Vocabulary:** names of jobs; talking about work; careers **Reading and listening activity:** *Applying for a job*
Revision and extension Units 13–18	

Self-study Workbook	Classroom Book

19 Narration

Grammar exercises
Listening: *Two stories*
Pronunciation: *Intonation: questions*
Reading: *Bad luck*

Talking about past events and their
circumstances; telling stories

Grammar: Past continuous tense; Past simple
tense; when & while

20 People

Vocabulary exercises
Listening: *Famous people*
Sound and spelling: *Long and short vowels*
Writing skills: *Relative clauses (1)*

Vocabulary: physical appearance; age; personal
characteristics

Reading and listening activity: *The Dream
Game*

21 Prediction

Grammar exercises
Listening: *Driving test*
Pronunciation: *Contrastive stress*
Reading: *Star gazing*

Making predictions; talking about
consequences

Grammar: will, won't & might; if/unless +
Present simple; going to

22 Around the world

Vocabulary exercises
Listening: *Living in a hot climate*
Sound and spelling: *Words with* s
Writing skills: *Relative clauses (2)*

Vocabulary: geographical features; weather
and climate; countries and nationalities

Reading and listening activity: *Car chaos*

23 Duration

Grammar exercises
Listening: *24 hours*
Pronunciation: *Dialogues*
Reading: *General knowledge quiz*

Talking about activities that are still going on;
asking and talking about duration

Grammar: Present perfect continuous and
simple; How long ...?; for & since; spend
(+ -ing)

24 But is it art?

Vocabulary exercises
Listening: *Choosing a painting*
Sound and spelling: *Words with* th
Writing skills: *Sequence (3)*

Vocabulary: art and literature; writers, artists
and performers

Reading and listening activity: *The Night in
the Hotel*

Revision and extension Units 19–24

1 Description

A There is(n't) & There are(n't)

Fill the gaps with expressions from the box.

Examples:

– *Is there* a dictionary?

– Yes, *there are* two on my desk.

there's	there are
there isn't	there aren't
is there	are there

1 .... a bottle of mineral water, but I'm afraid .... any glasses.

2 – .... a supermarket near here?

– No, ..., but .... a few small shops in the next street.

3 It's a terrible hotel. .... any curtains in the windows, ... a noisy

   discothèque next door, and .... only three bathrooms in the whole place.

4 – .... any good restaurants in this town?

– Yes, ... a very good fish restaurant near the station.

Short forms

There's a letter for you.   (= There is)

There isn't a phone in here.   (= There is not)

There aren't any good shops. (= There are not)

I've got three children.   (= have got)

It's got some lovely beaches.   (= has got)

They **haven't got** a car.   (= have not got)

It **hasn't got** central heating.   (= has not got)

B Have got

Rewrite these sentences using *have got*.

Examples:

There are some newspapers in the library. → *The library has got some newspapers.*

Is there a restaurant in this town?   → *Has this town got a restaurant?*

There isn't a phone in the office.   → *The office hasn't got a phone.*

1 There's a post office in the village.

....

2 Is there an ashtray in this car?

....

3 There isn't a window in the bathroom.

....

4 There aren't any lions in the zoo.

....

5 Are there carpets in the classrooms?

....

6 There's central heating in my office.

....

C Two descriptions

Here are pictures of two parts of a hotel. Write sentences describing them.

1 In the reception area ....
....
....
....
....
....
....
....

2 The bedroom's got ....
....
....
....
....
....
....
....

D Place prepositions

What are the missing words in sentences 1–9?
Write your answers in the diagram.

Then complete the missing word in
sentence 10 (going down).

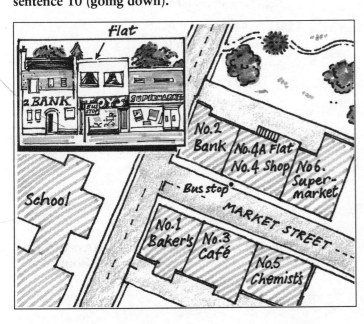

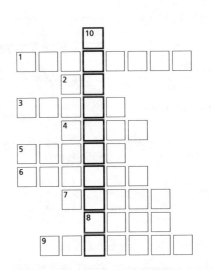

1 There's a café .... the flat.
2 The flat is .... Market Street.
3 The flat's .... a toyshop.
4 There's a bank .... to the flat.
5 There's a bus stop in .... of no. 4.
6 .... the flat, there's a park.
7 There's a toyshop .... the flat.
8 There's a school .... the flat.
9 The flat's .... a supermarket and a bank.
10 The flat's very .... for the shops.

TRANSLATION

Translate into your own language:

1 – Excuse me. Is there a phone near here?
– Yes, there's one by the reception desk.

....

....

2 – I like living near the University. There
are lots of bookshops, and there's a
good library too.

....

....

....

3 – Has the room got a shower?
– No, I'm afraid it hasn't, but there's
a bathroom at the end of the corridor.

....

....

....

Now cover up the left-hand side, and translate your sentences back into English.

LISTENING: Asking for help

You will hear three short conversations. Listen and answer
the questions.

1 The man is looking for a .... There's one

at the top of .... on the

.................................side. It's called The

.... Dragon ....

2 *a* The man is looking for a ....

Find it on the map:

....

b It's cheap/expensive.
large/small.
English/Italian.

c Which foods does the
woman mention?

meat   chicken   fish   bacon

eggs   cheese   chips   salad

3 *a* The woman is looking for a ....

b Mark these sentences T (true) or F (false):

.... It's in the town centre.

.... You can recognise it because it's white.

.... It's rather expensive.

.... It's called Eden Court.

.... The man recommends it.

PRONUNCIATION: Where's the stress?

1 Listen to these words on the tape.
Notice the main stress in each word.

airport	ticket	language
between	reply	about
telephone	facilities	recommend

2 Underline the main stress in these words.
Then listen to the tape.

office	information
computer	furniture
hotel	hungry
opposite	beside
café	understand

3 Look at these sentences. Where do you think
the main stress is?

a He hasn't got a ticket.
b I want to post a letter.
c Where's the bathroom?
d There's a policeman at the door.
e Are you a student here?
f How much food have we got?

Now listen to the tape. Then practise saying
the sentences.

DICTATION

You will hear parts of the three letters in *Good
points and bad points* (Classroom Book, page 9).
Listen and write down what you hear.

READING: Islands

Herm

Herm lies off the coast of France, and is one of the Channel Islands. It's very small – only about 2 square kilometres – and there are no cars, no buses, no bright lights and no nightclubs. The village is just a short walk from the harbour, and has a post office, a pub and a gift shop. The island's one hotel offers a sea view from most bedrooms.

From the village, you can walk all round the coast, or direct to Belvoir Bay across the middle of the island. Only 12 families live on Herm, but in summer there can be up to 2,000 day-visitors. Most of them stay on the beach, so on a busy day, it's best to go for a walk.

If it's not crowded Belvoir Bay is ideal for family swimming, low and sandy with a beach café. Herm's other beach is known as Shell Beach. It is made entirely of tiny bright shells, some washed up from as far away as Mexico.

Stromboli

The small Italian island of Stromboli is near Sicily, and is well-known because it has an active volcano. This may sound rather dangerous for the 400 inhabitants of the island. But in fact, although the volcano erupts every 10 minutes, it is quite safe.

In the north of the island there are two small villages next to each other – Santo Bartolo and Santo Vincenzo. They are peaceful places, with fine churches and small white houses which contrast with the black sand of the beaches.

In the south of the island, there is another small village, called Ginostra. It has only 30 inhabitants, mostly fishermen and their families. People say that Ginostra is the smallest port in the world – its harbour is only large enough to hold two fishing boats.

Most visitors to Stromboli come to look at the volcano. From Santo Bartolo there is a small path which leads up the side of the mountain. After about three or four hours you reach the top, and from here you can look straight down into the crater of the volcano.

1   **Which island is shown in the picture?**

   ....

2   **Look at the remarks in the table. Which island(s) do you think they are about? Write H or S.**

3   **What is the _main_ tourist attraction of**

   – Herm?

   ....

   – Stromboli?

   ....

   Choose from the following:

   walking   fine buildings
   beaches   a harbour
   fishing   a volcano

		H S
_a_	'It's a small island.'	H S
_b_	'What a beautiful church!'	S
_c_	'The harbour's incredibly small.'	
_d_	'There's only one village.'	
_e_	'There's a sandy beach.'	
_f_	'The beach is often very crowded.'	
_g_	'Are you _sure_ it's safe?'	
_h_	'You can walk right across the island.'	
_i_	'There aren't any cars.'	
_j_	'It's a long way to the top!'	

2 Family and friends

A Family tree

Complete this family tree with words from the box.
One of the words isn't used. Which one?

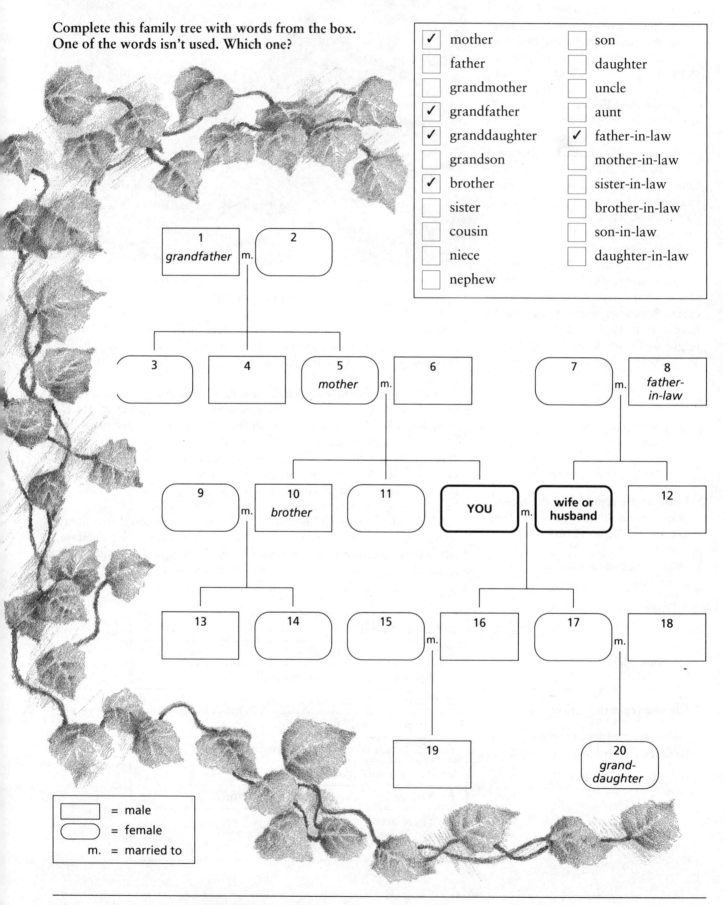

✔ mother	☐ son
☐ father	☐ daughter
☐ grandmother	☐ uncle
✔ grandfather	☐ aunt
✔ granddaughter	✔ father-in-law
☐ grandson	☐ mother-in-law
✔ brother	☐ sister-in-law
☐ sister	☐ brother-in-law
☐ cousin	☐ son-in-law
☐ niece	☐ daughter-in-law
☐ nephew	

1 *grandfather* m. 2

3   4   5 *mother* m. 6   7 m. 8 *father-in-law*

9 m. 10 *brother*   11   YOU m. wife or husband   12

13   14   15 m. 16   17 m. 18

19   20 *granddaughter*

☐ = male
⬭ = female
m. = married to

B Relationships

Fill the gaps with an expression from the box. Each expression is used *once.*

single
goes out with
engaged
married
get married
divorced
get divorced
pregnant

1 He .... Mary. She's his girlfriend.

2 She and her husband are very unhappy. They're going to ....

3 My brother is .... : he and his wife have 2 children. But I'm

....

4 She's .... : she's going to have a baby.

5 Jack's my fiancé: we're .... We're planning to ....

next summer.

6 She's .... now, but she still sees her ex-husband.

New words

Use this space to write down new words from the unit, with your own notes and examples.

....

....

....

....

....

....

....

....

....

....

....

....

....

TRANSLATION

Translate into your own language:

1 – Have you got any brothers or sisters?
   – Yes, I've got an older sister and a younger brother.

....
....
....

2 I'd like to introduce you to a friend of mine – Peter, this is Laura.

....
....

3 She's got a new boyfriend called George.

....

4 I'm in love with her, but she's in love with somebody else.

....
....

Now cover up the left-hand side, and translate your sentences back into English.

LISTENING: Relatives

You will hear four people talking about their relatives. Match the phrases in the box with the four relations.

five years older than me	very interested in life
104 years old	used to be rich
an airline pilot	nearly blind
lives in a small flat	very generous
lives in Canada	wears a wig
not very rich	often sends me presents
very poor	goes to interesting places

1 My grandmother ....
   ....
   ....
   ....

2 My brother ....
   ....
   ....
   ....

3 My uncle ....
   ....
   ....
   ....

4 My grandmother ....
   ....
   ....
   ....

SOUND AND SPELLING: Words with *a*

1 Listen to these words on the tape.
   Group A: /æ/ cat, man, apple, stand
   Group B: /eɪ/ came, later, table, play, waiter
   Group C: /ɑː/ start, large, ask, past, plant
   Group D: /ɔː/ fall, walk, war, autumn, draw
   Group E: /ɒ/ wash, want, watch

2 How do you say these words? Mark them A, B, C, D or E. Then listen to the tape.

3
☐ name		☐ day
☐ small		☐ warm
☐ faster		☐ station
☐ happy		☐ catch
☐ train		☐ talk
☐ hard		☐ what

You will hear four sentences. Cover this page, and write them down.

DICTATION

You will hear part of the text from *Love Story* (Classroom Book, page 13).

Listen and write down what you hear.

WRITING SKILLS: Sentences

1 A *sentence* begins with a *capital letter* and usually ends with a *full stop*.

How many sentences are there in this paragraph?

....

> I have two brothers and a sister. My older brother works in a factory. My younger brother is only 14, and is still at school. My sister is the oldest. She is married, and teaches at the local primary school.

2 **This paragraph is badly written. Rewrite it so that it has *four* sentences.**

> I have no brothers or sisters. But I have two cousins. One of them is younger than me. And the other is older. The younger one is 19. And has just started university, the older one is married, and lives with her family in Australia.

3 **This paragraph has too many sentences. Improve it by joining some sentences together.**

> I have one sister. She is older than me. She is studying to be a doctor. My father is a shopkeeper. He has two sisters. One is retired. She lives in Scotland. The other lives in London. She works in a children's hospital.

4 **Now write a short paragraph about some of the people in your own family.**

3 Habits, customs and facts

A Simple verbs

All the answers are verbs in the Present simple tense.

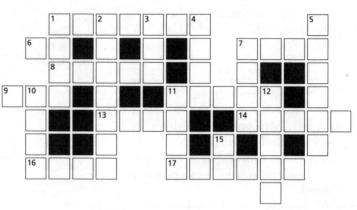

▶ **Across clues**

1 John often .... the late film on Fridays. (7)
6 I usually .... the washing up after lunch. (2)
7 On Mother's Day I always .... my mother some flowers. (4)
8 At 11 o'clock, she sits down with a cup of coffee and .... the newspaper. (5)
9 When I'm lost I always .... a policeman. (3)
11 Travels by air. (5)
13 They usually .... dinner at about 8 o'clock. (4)
14 They .... all their money on clothes. (5)
16 He always .... his homework before dinner. (4)
17 When people are bored, they often .... their watches. (4, 2)

▼ **Down clues**

1 I'm a secretary. I .... in a bank. (4)
2 My mother .... French in the local school. (7)
3 He always .... a party on his birthday. (3)
4 They've got a shop. They .... furniture. (4)
5 Starts. (6)
7 She .... to work on her motorbike. (4)
10 People usually .... cards at Christmas. (4)
11 I always .... tired at the end of the week. (4)
12 In Brazil, they .... Portuguese. (5)
15 We usually .... out on Saturday night. (2)

B Do(es)(n't)

Fill the gaps with *do*, *does*, *don't* or *doesn't*.

1 – Excuse me. .... this bus go to the town centre?

– No, it .... You want the number 14 or the number 23. But they .... stop at this bus-stop, I'm afraid.

2 – Why .... Prince Charles carry a red, white and blue umbrella?

– To keep the rain off.

3 – .... you smoke?

– No, I ...., thanks. But you can if you like. It .... bother me.

4 – How much money .... he earn? .... you know?

– Yes, I .... Why .... you want to know?

– Well, he's my brother. But he .... tell me anything.

> **Present simple tense**
>
> Negative: **don't/doesn't** + infinitive
> – He **doesn't** like football.
> – I **don't** drive a car.
>
> Questions: **do/does** + subject + infinitive
> – **Do** you read a newspaper?
> – Where **does** she work?

C Asking Wh- questions

Rewrite these questions as Wh- questions. Use question words from the box.

How	How much	What	What time
When		Where	Why

Example:

Does it cost £5? £8? £15? → *How much does it cost?*

1 Does she park her car in a garage? on the street? in a car park?

....

2 Do crocodiles eat fish? plants? people?

....

3 Do you have lunch at 1 o'clock? 1.30? 2 o'clock?

....

4 Do you want to pay in cash? by credit card? by cheque?

....

5 Does he walk to work because he enjoys it? because he hasn't got a car? because it's good exercise?

....

6 Do you use your English at work? at home? on holiday?

....

D Frequency

The sentences below aren't true. Rewrite them with different frequency expressions.

Examples:

Politicians *never* lie.   → *Politicians sometimes lie.*

People *usually* go to work on Sundays. → *People don't usually go to work on Sundays.*

1 It *never* rains in California.

....

2 The sun *doesn't usually* rise in the east.

....

3 Businessmen *don't* wear suits *very often*.

....

4 Siberia is *sometimes* cold in winter.

....

5 People *always* wear sweaters in bed.

....

6 Students *often* go to sleep in class.

....

TRANSLATION

Translate into your own language:

1 – What do you do?
  – I'm a secretary. I work for Esso.

....

....

2 – Do you usually have a cooked meal
    in the evening?
  – No, not usually. Only at weekends.

....

....

....

3 The hotel closes in October, but it
  opens again for Christmas and the
  New Year.

....

....

....

Now cover up the left-hand side, and translate your sentences back into English.

LISTENING: Japanese New Year

You will hear someone talking about what people do at New Year in Japan. Here are some of the things that happen. Listen, and put them in the right order:

☐ They put on special clothes.

☐ Everyone cleans the house.

☐ Bells ring 108 times.

1 Housewives prepare special food.

☐ They eat a special meal.

☐ They go to a shrine.

☐ They wish each other a Happy New Year.

☐ They drink rice wine.

☐ They watch television.

PRONUNCIATION: The sound /ə/

1 Listen to the sound /ə/ on the tape. It is only used in *unstressed* syllables.

2 Listen to these words. Each circle marks a /ə/ sound.

brother   the teacher   often
about   forget   information
policeman   American   a computer

3 Put a circle round the /ə/ sounds in these words. Then listen to the tape.

a woman	breakfast
an actor	never
grandfather	the winter

4 Look at these sentences. Underline the main stress, and circle the /ə/ sounds.

  a My brother's a famous actor.
  b In the summer he works in a factory.
  c Does she read a newspaper?
  d I never visit my relations.
  e The town centre's busy today.

Now listen to the tape. Then practise saying the sentences.

DICTATION

You will hear one of the texts from *Cultural differences* (Classroom Book, page 18).

Listen and write down what you hear.

READING: Reptiles and amphibians

Match the descriptions with the animals. Which of the six animals is not described?

1 ....s live in tropical rivers and lakes. They spend the night in the water and come out to lie in the sun during the day. They eat animals and birds that come to the water's edge to drink. After catching its prey in its mouth, the .... first drowns it by holding it under water, and then eats it. ....s also eat large stones, which help them to balance when they are in the water.

2 ....s are usually between 15 and 30 cm long. Most live in forests in Africa. They have very long thin tongues which they use to catch flying insects. ....s may be green, yellow or brown, and they can quickly change the colour of their skin and so become almost invisible against their surroundings.

3 ....s spend most of their time in the sea. They only come onto land every two or three years, to lay their eggs; to do this they always return to the beach where they were born. The female lays her eggs in a hole in the sand, then covers it and leaves. Two months later, the eggs hatch and the baby ....s must find their own way back to the sea.

4 The .... is completely adapted to living in the sea, and never goes on land. If it is washed onto the shore it cannot move and soon dies. It breathes air, but it can stay under water for up to two hours. The .... feeds on fish and it is very poisonous.

5 The .... lives on the land along the edges of lakes and streams. It is most active at night, when it eats insects, fish and sometimes small birds. Every spring, the female lays between 10,000 and 20,000 eggs, which float to the surface of the water, but only a few of these survive to become adult. The .... is a very good jumper. It can jump as far as two metres.

Adapted from the *Longman Illustrated Animal Encyclopedia*

A Sea Snake

B Bullfrog

C Chameleon

D Gecko

E Turtle

F Crocodile

4 Going places

A Public opinions

Look at these remarks about public transport. Which adjective goes best with each remark?

1 'The seats are very hard, especially on a long journey.' ....

2 'I can't understand why it costs so much.' ....

3 'They're always on time.' ....

4 'It's difficult to find a seat during the rush hour.' ....

5 'They seem to have a lot of accidents.' ....

6 'It stops at every little station on the way.' ....

7 'Sometimes they come, and sometimes they don't.' ....

8 'The important thing is that everyone can afford the fare.' ....

| comfortable |
| uncomfortable |
| cheap |
| expensive |
| fast |
| slow |
| safe |
| dangerous |
| empty |
| crowded |
| reliable |
| unreliable |

B Rail, road and air

Write the missing words in the diagram.

Travelling by rail: 1–7 ▶

You can buy your ticket at the ticket (1). Your ticket can be single (one-way) or (2) (two-way).
Excuse me. Where's the nearest underground (3)?
The (6) leaves at 11.05 from (5) three. Don't be late, because it always leaves on (4).
It's very busy at the weekend, so it's a good idea to reserve a (7).

Travelling by road: 8–14 ▶

There's your bus, standing at the bus (8). You'd better run if you want to (1) it.
The tank's nearly empty. We'd better stop at a (13) station and (9) it up.
Most children know how to ride a (11).
When you get on the bus, tell the (12) that you want to go to the university. He or she will tell you when to get (14).

Travelling by air: 15–21 ▶

The plane (15) off at 9.00 and lands at 11.30.
Will all (16) please fasten their seat (18)?
You should get to the (17) at least one hour before your (19), so that you have time to (20) in your baggage.
If you need anything, ask a (21) or a (21)ess.

Now read the words going down ▼ to complete this sentence:

You can use rail, road and air to get ....

C Journeys

Write about two regular journeys that you make. Use expressions from the box. Example:

I go to work by underground. I usually leave at 8.30. The journey takes about 25 minutes, and I get to the office at about 9 o'clock. It costs £2 for a return ticket.

I (often/usually/sometimes) go to ...... by ......
...... leave ...... at ......
...... reach / arrive at / get to ...... at ......
The journey takes ......
It costs ......

1 ....

....

....

....

....

2 ....

....

....

....

....

New words

Use this space to write down new words from the unit, with your own notes and examples.

TRANSLATION

Translate into your own language:

1 – How do you get to work?
  – I usually drive, but sometimes I go by bus.

....
....
....

2 We always buy a few things in the duty-free shop.

....
....

3 The journey takes about two hours.

....

4 Hurry up, or we'll miss the train.

....

Now cover up the left-hand side, and translate your sentences back into English.

LISTENING: Likes and dislikes

You will hear four people talking about how much they like travelling:

1 by plane   2 by train   3 by bus   4 by car

1 *Before you listen:*
   Here are some of the things they say. Which form of transport do you think they are talking about? Write P(lane), T(rain), B(us) or C(ar).

P	I get very frightened.
	It takes forever to get somewhere.
	I don't like it when they take off.
	I find it very convenient.
	I can listen to the radio.
	It's a perfect opportunity to read a book.
	Usually you can't even sit down.
	I get very bored.
	I can get from A to B exactly.
	I have to hold somebody's hand.

2 **Now listen to the tape, and check your answers.**

SOUND AND SPELLING: Words with *e*

1 **Listen to these words on the tape.**

Group A: /e/ bed, letter, sell, head, weather
Group B: /iː/ meat, teacher, week, cheese
Group C: /ɜː/ her, hers, verb, learn, earth
Group D: /uː/ new, stew, flew
Group E: /ɪ/ boxes, waited, reply, kitchen, before

2 **How do you say these words? Mark them A, B, C, D or E. Then listen to the tape.**

	few		sleep
	yellow		dress
	earn		early
	ready		horses
	jeans		market
	beside		forget

3 **You will hear four sentences. Cover this page, and write them down.**

DICTATION

You will hear one of the texts from *How to get there* (Classroom Book, page 21).

Listen and write down what you hear.

WRITING SKILLS: Punctuation

1 Look at these sentences:

We usually go to church on Sundays.
Does Mary speak French?
I just love Italy in the spring!

Notice how we use these *punctuation marks* **to end a sentence:**

. *(full stop)*   ? *(question mark)*   ! *(exclamation mark)*

Notice that we use *capital letters*:

– at the beginning of a sentence
– for names of people and places
– for days and months
– for languages
– with the word *I*

2 Look at these words. Which ones should have capital letters?

ernest hemingway	today	summer	tuesday
german	october	london	the mountains
village	the alps	language school	can i go now?
the oxford school of english			

3 Each sentence has *two* **mistakes. Correct them.**

a he speaks german but not Italian.   ....

b Does this Train go to Moscow   ....

c The meeting will be on friday, 14th May   ....

d can i get there by bus?   ....

4 This paragraph should contain *eight* **sentences. Rewrite it, adding punctuation and capital letters.**

my sister has got a new bike and she spends nearly all her time on it every afternoon she comes home from school and quickly has something to eat then she goes out on her bike and cycles round the streets until it gets dark i never see her at weekends because she spends all day riding her bike in the evenings she reads magazines about cycling it's her birthday next week do you know what i'm going to give her i'm going to give her a mirror for her bike

....
....
....
....
....
....
....
....
....
....
....

5 Now

A Cross -ing words

Write the missing *-ing* forms in the diagram.

-ing forms: spelling rules

stand (+ ing) → standing
change (¢ + ing) → changing
sit (+ t + ing) → sitting

▶ **Across clues**

2 – Hey! Where are you ....?
    – Home. It's late. (5)
4 I think they're .... tennis in the park. (7)
7 Could you phone back later? He's ....
    a bath at the moment. (6)
9 We're not losing – we're ....! (7)
11 – Are you ready yet?
    – Nearly. I'm just .... into
    some clean clothes. (8)
12 I'm .... a fresh pot
    of coffee. Would you
    like some? (6)
13 – Why's that man
    ....?
    – He's trying to
    catch that
    bus. (7)

▼ **Down clues**

1 You're
    .... an
    exercise on *-ing*
    forms. (5)
3 She's got a headache.
    She's .... down
    upstairs. (5)
5 They can't find a flat, so
    they're .... with her
    parents. (6)
6 Look. It's stopped raining. The
    sun's .... (7)
8 The bell's .... The lesson's finished. (7)
10 They're .... very quietly. I can't hear what
    they're saying. (7)
11 – I wonder where they are.
    – Here they are – they're .... through the door now. (6)

B Simple or continuous?

Fill the gaps with a verb from the box, in the Present simple or the Present
continuous tense. Use each verb twice.

| have |
| stay |
| teach |
| wash |
| wear |
| write |

1 That's her, over there. She .... a green jacket.

2 He's in the bathroom. I think he .... his hair.

3 We usually .... with friends, but they're away, so we

.... in a hotel.

4 – Can I speak to the manager, please?

   – I'm sorry. She .... lunch at the moment.

5 I cook the meals, and my flat-mate .... the dishes.

6 She's a schoolteacher. She .... maths.

7 He spends all his time in his room. He says he .... a novel.

8 I .... glasses for driving and watching TV.

9 At the moment, I .... in the local school, but it's not a permanent job.

10 On Sundays, they .... breakfast in bed.

11 They don't visit me very often, but they .... every week.

C Asking Wh- questions

Rewrite these questions as *Wh-* questions.
Use question words from the box.

Example:

Are you studying maths? Chinese? History?
What are you studying?

Who	How
What	How many
Why	Where

1 Are they staying at a hotel? at a friend's house? at a campsite?

....

2 Is she talking to her brother? cousin? sister?

....

3 Is the baby crying because he's unhappy? because he's hungry? because he's tired?

....

4 Are you reading a novel? a guide book? a grammar book?

....

5 Are you feeling happy? excited? tired?

....

6 Is she wearing one ring? two rings? three rings?

....

D There is/are + -ing

You're on the phone at a party. Describe what you can see using *There is/are + -ing*.

Examples:

You can see a man. He's wearing a white suit. → *There's a man wearing a white suit.*
Two men are fighting. They're in a corner. → *There are two men fighting in a corner.*

1 You can see some people in the kitchen. They're eating.

....

2 There are two children. They're sitting on the stairs.

....

3 You can see a woman. She's playing the piano.

....

4 Two people are dancing. They're on a table.

....

5 Some people are outside. They're trying to get in.

....

6 You can see a disc jockey. He's playing loud music.

....

TRANSLATION

Translate into your own language:

1 Sorry, I can't come now. I'm helping my brother mend his car.

....
....

2 Look – there's a man lying in the middle of the road.

....
....

3 – What's Lisa doing these days?
   – I don't know. I don't see her very often.

....
....
....

Now cover up the left-hand side, and translate your sentences back into English.

LISTENING: These days

You will hear two people saying what they are doing these days. Listen and complete the table. Write ✓ or ✗.

Is she/he	Woman	Man
1 very busy?		
2 studying for an exam?		
3 preparing for visitors?		
4 reading a novel?		
5 moving mattresses?		
6 looking after a sick child?		
7 looking for a new house?		
8 looking for a job?		

PRONUNCIATION: Reduced vowels (1)

1 Listen to the words in the box. Their sound changes to /ə/ when they are not stressed.

at	at six o'clock
for	for five hours
of	a packet of tea
to	to the cinema
from	from Japan
some	some coffee
and	brothers and sisters
them	I don't like them

2 Listen to these sentences. Each one contains *one* word from the box. Write the word you hear.

a ....   *g* ....

b ....   *h* ....

c ....   *i* ....

d ....   *j* ....

e ....   *k* ....

f ....   *l* ....

Now listen again, and practise saying the sentences.

DICTATION

You will hear three of the texts in *Around now* (Classroom Book, page 25).

Listen and write down what you hear.

READING: What's going on?

Here are the first sentences of three different paragraphs:

Paragraph A The weather's terrible today.

Paragraph B It's Saturday evening.

Paragraph C It's a beautiful day.

Here are some other sentences from the three paragraphs. Which paragraphs do they belong to?
Write A, B or C by each one.

1 ☐ The parks and children's playgrounds are all empty.

2 ☐ There are long queues outside cinemas and theatres.

3 ☐ Strong winds are making driving difficult, and the police are asking drivers to drive slowly.

4 ☐ Windows are open, and people are sitting outside on their balconies.

5 ☐ The streets are full of parked cars, and drivers looking for a place to park.

6 ☐ It's pouring with rain and in some places it's snowing.

7 ☐ There's a lot of washing hanging out to dry.

8 ☐ Everyone's wearing sandals and short-sleeved shirts.

9 ☐ There are crowds of people walking along the streets or standing around in small groups.

10 ☐ There are a lot of people standing in shop doorways to keep dry.

11 ☐ Everyone's carrying umbrellas and wearing raincoats.

12 ☐ The parks are full of people lying on the grass.

13 ☐ Most shops are shut, but the bars and restaurants are doing a lot of business.

14 ☐ The sun's shining, and there isn't a cloud in the sky.

Food and drink

A Kinds of food

In each puzzle, answer 12 (going down) is a kind of shop, and
answers 1–11 (going across) are things you can buy there.

Puzzle 1

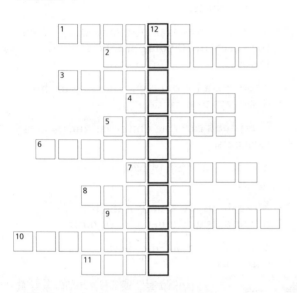

Puzzle 2

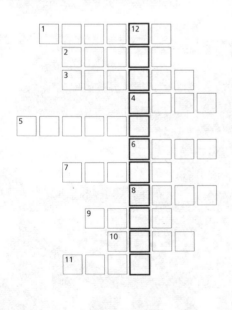

B Talking about food

Fill the gaps with suitable words from the box.
Some words are used more than once.

serves	kind of	reserve	order	need
served	made from	cooked	dish	bill

1 Tortilla is a .... omelette, which comes from Spain. To make it, you .... eggs, potatoes and herbs. The omelette is .... in a large pan. It can be .... hot or cold.

2 It's my favourite restaurant. I always sit at the same table, and the same waiter always .... me. I always .... the same .... too: tagliatelle. It's always very good. When the .... comes, it's always for the same amount; and I always leave a large tip. And I never have to .... my table before I come.

3 – Are you ready to .... now, sir?

– Um ... what's Rogan Josh?

– It's an Indian .... It's .... lamb and tomatoes, and it's usually .... with rice. It's rather hot and dry.

– Mm. I think I'll try it, please.

New words

Use this space to write down new words from the unit, with your own notes and examples.

....
....
....
....
....
....
....
....
....
....
....
....
....
....

TRANSLATION

Translate into your own language:

1 Could we have the bill, please?

....

2 This dish is made from fish and vegetables, and it also has some spices in it.

....

....

3 Would you like something to drink?

....

4 I'd like half a kilo of potatoes, a packet of butter and a small can of tomatoes.

....

....

....

Now cover up the left-hand side, and translate your sentences back into English.

LISTENING: Polish dishes

You will hear a Polish woman talking about two typical dishes from Poland: *bigos* and *chlodnik*. Listen and answer the questions.

1 Which ingredients are for *bigos*? Which are for *chlodnik*? (Write *b* or *c*).

[C] beetroot	[ ] eggs	[ ] meat
[ ] tomatoes	[ ] cream	[ ] bacon
[ ] cabbage	[ ] spices	[ ] beetroot leaves

2 Which dish:

– is a kind of soup? ....

– is usually eaten cold? ....

– tastes better the next day? ....

– is good to eat in summer? ....

SOUND AND SPELLING: Words with *i*

1 Listen to these words on the tape.

Group A: /ɪ/ sit, ticket, insect, sister, give
Group B: /aɪ/ white, like, night, high, tie
Group C: /ɜː/ skirt, birthday, girl
Group D: /iː/ believe, piece, receive

2 How do you say these words? Mark them A, B, C or D. Then listen to the tape.

[ ]	drink	[ ]	field
[ ]	shirt	[ ]	right
[ ]	different	[ ]	swimming
[ ]	write	[ ]	library
[ ]	first	[ ]	bird
[ ]	die	[ ]	with

3 You will hear four sentences. Cover this page, and write them down.

DICTATION

You will hear most of the dialogue from *Eating out* (Classroom Book, page 29 and page 125).

Listen and write down what you hear.

WRITING SKILLS: Reference

1 Look at these examples.
   What do the words in *italic type* refer to?

a That's my sister. *She*'s sitting in the corner.
   Come with me and I'll introduce you to *her*.

b John went to the grocer's to buy some eggs.
   On the way home, *he* dropped *them* and *they*
   broke.

c The two men were in the next room. *They* stayed
   there for about half an hour. Then *they* came out
   and said, "We're ready."

d – Do you like Rome?
   – Yes, I think *it*'s a beautiful city. I often go *there*
   on business.

She/her	=	*my sister*
he	=	....
them/they	=	....
They/they	=	....
there	=	....
it	=	....
there	=	....

2 Fill each gap with a word from the box.

he	she	they	it	there
him	her	them		

a – Do you know London?

   – Yes, I know .... very well. I live ....!

b My sister's bought a new flat. .... isn't very big, but .... likes ....

c I hope my brother's all right. I wrote to .... a month ago, but .... didn't reply.

d – Those are nice trousers. Can I try .... on?

   – Yes, OK - but I don't think ....'re your size.

e – Does Paula still work in that café?

   – I don't think so. I was .... yesterday, and I didn't see ....

3 What's wrong with this story? Rewrite it using words from the box above.

A new restaurant opened in town last week, so I decided to go to the restaurant to see what the restaurant was like. After a few minutes a waitress came over to the table and gave me a menu, but the waitress wasn't very friendly. I ordered chicken and chips. Half an hour later, the waitress brought the food. The food wasn't very good. The chicken was tough, and the chicken had a rather strange taste. The chips were even worse; the chips were half cold and very greasy. I couldn't eat the chips at all.

   I called the waitress and asked the waitress to bring me the bill. The bill came to £25. I asked to see the manager. I told the manager that I thought £25 was too much for such a bad meal. I gave the manager £5, and then walked out of the restaurant. I'll certainly never go to the restaurant again.

....

....

....

....

....

....

....

....

....

....

....

....

....

....

....

Revision and extension

1 Verb forms

Write the correct form of the verbs.

Example:

He *likes* (like) chocolate cake.

1 .... (be) there any other foreigners at this party, or .... (be) I the only one?

2 Let me type those letters. I .... (*not* – have got) anything else to do.

3 She must be very rich: she .... (drive) a Mercedes and she .... (have got) an enormous house.

4 My uncle .... (live) in California, but at the moment he .... (stay) with some friends in Rome.

5 I .... (study) French at the moment, but I still .... (*not* – speak) it very well.

2 Asking questions

Complete the questions.

Example:

– Where *do you come from*?
– From Canberra. We're Australian.

1 – How many ....?
  – They've got three – two girls and a boy.

2 – What .... these days?
  – Nothing much – I'm still looking for a job.

3 – What time ....?
  – Oh, he usually gets home at about 6.30.

4 – Where ....?
  – At the General Hospital. I'm a nurse.

5 – .... a bank near here?
  – Yes there is, but I'm afraid they're all closed today.

6 – Why .... that heavy coat?
  – Because I feel cold – that's why!

7 – ....?
  – Yes I do. But only about 10 a day.

3 Prepositions

Fill the gaps with prepositions from the box.

1 I'll meet you .... the station.

2 Please don't stand in front .... me. I can't see.

3 Unfortunately there's only a thin wall .... my room and theirs.

4 I'd like to invite you .... my birthday party.

5 What do you usually have .... breakfast?

6 We're staying .... home this evening.

7 The bus gets .... the airport .... 6.30.

8 The trains always run .... time.

of	with	between
for	at	to
by	on	

9 Would you like to sit .... this table .... the window?

10 Why don't you go .... train? It's quicker.

11 Are you still going out .... that singer?

4 Word order

Put these jumbled sentences in the right order. Remember to begin each sentence with a capital letter.

Example: me often presents grandparents send my .
My grandparents often send me presents.

1 in there children river the swimming some are .

....

2 have bill we please could the ?

....

3 live centre do town near you the ?

....

4 usually the I radio news to on the listen .

....

5 your shower got bathroom you a in have ?

....

6 the often they cinema very go to don't .

....

5 Writing paragraphs

Write a short paragraph (2 or 3 sentences) on the following:

1 Who uses the kitchen in your house? What do they do there?

....

....

....

2 What do you usually have for breakfast?

....

....

....

3 What are the bus services like where you live?

....

....

....

4 Look out of the window. What's happening?

....

....

....

7 The past

A Irregular squares

All the answers are in the past tense. They are all irregular verbs.

Irregular verbs
There's a list of irregular verbs at the back of the book.

1▼ She jumped off the boat and .... to shore. (4)
2▶ I liked them. They .... very nice. (4)
3▼ He .... his bicycle to the shops. (4)
4▶ She .... a phone call. (4)

1▶ Yesterday the weather .... very cold. (3)
1▼ I .... them a letter. (5)
2▼ He .... for eight hours last night. (5)
3▶ I .... up at 7.00 this morning. (4)
4▶ She .... the party early and went home. (4)

1▶ He .... the ball over the wall. (5)
2▼ I .... a bath before I got dressed this morning. (3)
3▼ I .... out last night. (4)
4▶ They .... some mineral water with their meal. (5)

1▼ She .... a new car six months ago. (6)
2▼ He .... me a telegram. (4)
3▶ I .... a suit to the wedding. (4)
4▼ She .... me a record for my birthday. (4)
5▶ The cat .... a mouse, and brought it to show me. (6)
6▶ After taking the medicine, I .... much better. (4)

B Positive and negative

Bella and her husband Dick never do the same things on the same day. For example, yesterday

Bella *listened* to the radio.
Dick *didn't listen* to the radio.

What else happened (or didn't happen) yesterday?

1 Dick didn't have a bath.

  Bella ....

2 Bella went to the shops.

  Dick ....

3 Dick made a cake.

  Bella ....

4 Bella didn't watch television.

  Dick ....

5 Dick didn't read the newspaper.

  Bella ....

6 Bella didn't lose her umbrella.

  Dick ....

7 Dick took the dog for a walk.

  Bella ....

8 Dick didn't drive to work.

  Bella ....

C Asking Wh- questions

Rewrite these questions as Wh- questions.
Use question words from the box.

Example:

Did you ask John to dinner? Jane? Alice?
Who did you ask to dinner?

What	How
When	How much
Why	Where
Who	

1 Did they go to a restaurant last night? a theatre? a cinema?

....

2 Did he leave because he was bored? because he was ill? because he had another appointment?

....

3 Did you spend £5? £10? £20?

....

4 Did she say 'Hello'? 'Go away'? 'Goodbye'?

....

5 Did your mother arrive yesterday? two days ago? last week?

....

6 Did you get in with a key? by ringing the bell? by breaking a window?

....

D Time expressions

Fill the gaps with *at, on, in, ago* or ✗ (= nothing).
Examples:

I posted that letter ..*at*... nine o'clock ..*in*... the

morning ..*on*... 4th July 1988. It arrived ...*✗*.... this

morning. I posted another letter ...*✗*.... yesterday – just 24 hours .*ago*.. – to the same address, and it arrived

..*at*... the same time!

> **Time prepositions**
> at: **at 6 o'clock, at midday**
> on: **on Monday, on 3rd April**
> in: **in the morning, in May, in spring, in 1920**
> No preposition: **last year, last week, yesterday**

1 My parents got married .... 1941. They met .... one o'clock in the morning .... January 1st, got engaged .... February, and got married .... April. Just think – that happened more than 50 years ....

2 Ken moved to Paris 10 years ...., and .... last Tuesday he visited the Louvre for the first time.

3 I travelled a lot .... last week. .... Monday I had two important meetings – one .... the morning in New York and another .... 10 .... the evening in Washington. Then .... Wednesday I flew to Tokyo, and then on to Hong Kong .... Friday morning. I only got back to the States .... yesterday morning.

4 Linda didn't feel well when she woke up .... this morning. She went to work, but left .... 12.30, and went to see the doctor .... this afternoon. I saw her about half an hour ...., and she looked quite ill.

TRANSLATION

Translate into your own language:

1 – Did you find your watch?
   – Yes, I found it yesterday, but then
     I lost it again.

....

....

....

2 – When did you last ride a bike?
   – About three years ago.

....

....

3 The baby was born at five o'clock
  in the morning on Friday 17th
  February.

....

....

....

Now cover up the left-hand side, and translate your sentences back into English.

LISTENING: When did you last...?

You will hear people answering these questions:

A When did you last cook a meal?
B When did you last drink champagne?
C When did you last go to the dentist?
D When did you last sing a song in public?

1 *Before you listen:* Look at these phrases. Which speaker do you think uses each one?

☐ D It was out in the street.
☐   They had a party afterwards.
☐   All my teeth were in fine condition.
☐   I ate it about half an hour later.
☐   I'd had a very good time.
☐   Fried eggs on toast.
☐   I needed no work done.
☐   I'd been to a friend's party.
☐   I got in quite late.
☐   At a friend's wedding.
☐   I was very happy.

Now listen to the tape, and check your answers.

2 Listen again. When did each thing happen?

He last cooked a meal ....

He last drank champagne ....

She last went to the dentist ....

He last sang a song in public ....

PRONUNCIATION: Reduced vowels (2)

1 Listen to the words in the box. Their sound often changes to /ə/ when they are unstressed.

are	My friends are here.
was	He was very hungry.
were	Where were you last night?
do	What do penguins eat?
does	What does that mean?
can	I can dance the Polka.

2 Listen to these sentences. Each one contains *one* word from the box.
  Write the word you hear.

a .... g ....
b .... h ....
c .... i ....
d .... j ....
e .... k ....
f .... l ....

Now listen again, and practise saying the sentences.

DICTATION

You will hear one of the texts from *Famous firsts* (Classroom Book, page 34).

Listen and write down what you hear.

READING: Jokes

Can you finish these jokes? Choose the best five lines from the box.

1 A man was walking in a park when he saw a young girl playing with a large dog. He went up to them and asked the girl 'Does your dog bite?'

'Of course not,' said the girl. The man smiled at the dog and held out his hand, and immediately the dog bit him.
'Ow!' he shouted. 'I thought you said your dog didn't bite!'
'It doesn't,' the girl replied. '...........................'

2 A woman went to have her eyes tested. The optician told her to sit down and look at a board which had some letters written on it.

'Now' said the optician, 'can you read the top letter?'
'No,' replied the woman.
The optician held it closer. 'Can you read it now?' he asked.
'No.'
He held it closer still. 'Can you read it now?'
'No,' replied the woman.
'Oh dear,' said the optician. 'This is serious.'
'I know,' said the woman. '...........................'

3 A man went to a restaurant and ordered lunch. When the food came, it was terrible, and the man couldn't eat it. He called the waiter and said

'Waiter, this food's terrible! I want to see the manager!'
'Sorry,' the waiter replied. '...........................'

a My eyes are terrible.
b It's getting late.
c Shall I call an ambulance?
d No, yes, no, yes, no, yes, no.
e I can't read.
f That isn't my dog.
g I can't hear you very well.
h She's just gone out to lunch.
i No, it isn't.
j Now we're going to the cinema.

4 One morning a man found a penguin outside his front door. He took the penguin to the police station, and the policeman told him to take it to the zoo. That evening, the policeman came out of

the police station and saw the man and the penguin waiting at a bus stop.
'Hey,' he said. 'I thought I told you to take that penguin to the zoo.'
'I did,' the man replied, '...........................'

5 A man was driving his son to school. He turned left, and the driver behind them hooted at them.

Then they turned right, and another driver shouted at them.
'I wonder if my indicators are working,' said the man, and he stopped the car and asked his son to get out. Then he turned on his left indicator and called 'Well? Is it working?' and the son called back, '...........................'

Somewhere to live

A Phrases

Complete these sentences with a suitable phrase. For each phrase use one item from Box A and one from Box B (e.g. *the city + centre = the city centre*).

Example:

The trouble with living in *the city centre* is that you can never find a place to park your car.

A	B
a detached	~~centre~~
a main	floor
a view	house
block	north
faces	of flats
looks out	of the sea
~~the city~~	on a park
the ninth	road

1 They live on the coast. Their living room window has

....

2 I hope the lift's working: he lives on ....!

3 We live in ...., so we don't hear our neighbours' TV.

4 Our bedroom window ...., so it doesn't get much sun.

5 We get a lot of traffic noise: we live on ....

6 Our balcony .... – it's a very pleasant place to sit.

7 I live right at the top of a tall ....

B Furniture and fittings

There are 22 words hidden in the square. Words can run in any direction: forward, backward, up, down, and diagonally. See if you can find:

1 two kinds of table

   coffee

   ....

2 five things that use running water

   ....

3 four things that use electricity or gas

   ....

4 four pieces of furniture to sit or lie on

   ....

5 something on the floor and something on the windows

   ....

6 somewhere to sit and work

   ....

7 two places to keep things (with doors)

   ....

8 two things you might put on the wall

   ....

T	P	M	A	L	D	I	N	I	N	G
E	P	I	C	U	P	B	O	A	R	D
P	F	R	I	D	G	E	E	K	E	N
R	O	R	E	W	O	H	S	D	E	I
A	T	O	I	L	E	T	O	C	F	S
C	U	R	T	A	I	N	S	O	F	A
S	E	V	L	E	H	S	K	O	O	B
I	P	R	I	A	H	C	H	K	C	H
N	Y	L	I	G	H	T	M	E	U	S
K	S	E	D	E	A	O	E	R	Z	A
E	D	W	E	B	O	R	D	R	A	W

C What are they like?

Choose adjectives from the box which could describe:

bare	quiet
convenient	spacious
dark	sunny
noisy	untidy

1 a house near an airport ....

2 a house on a hillside facing south ....

3 a room with a lot of things lying on the floor ....

4 a house with shops and school nearby ....

5 a house with very small windows ....

6 a room with very little furniture ....

7 a house in a street with very little traffic ....

8 a house with large rooms ....

New words

Use this space to write down new words from the unit, with your own notes and examples.

....

....

....

....

....

....

....

....

....

....

....

....

....

TRANSLATION

Translate into your own language:

1 – Where is your flat exactly?
   – It's on the third floor, opposite
     the lift.

....
....
....

2 We haven't got any furniture yet,
   so the room looks a bit empty.

....
....

3 We're living with my parents at
   the moment, but we're hoping to
   move into a flat soon.

....
....
....

Now cover up the left-hand side, and translate your sentences back into English.

LISTENING: Favourite rooms

You will hear two people talking about their favourite room.

1 Listen and choose the correct words in this text:

In my room, I play | loud / quiet | music on the | piano / stereo | .

Because the room is | big / small | , it is | easy / difficult | to

keep warm. The room has a | big / small | window,

which I | often open / keep closed | in summer | and then / because | the

neighbours complain about the music.

2 **Find nine factual differences between this text and what you hear:**

My sister's bedroom is the smallest room in the house. It is full of things which she does not let me touch. The room has a metal bed, and no other furniture. There's a shelf beside the bed, and it is full of books, which she has collected for five years. It's got a big window, which I don't like very much. The room is so full of things that it is difficult to clean.

1 ....   6 ....

2 ....   7 ....

3 ....   8 ....

4 ....   9 ....

5 ....

SOUND AND SPELLING: Words with *o* (1)

1 Listen to these words on the tape.

Group A: /ɒ/ hot, lost, socks, shopping
Group B: /əʊ/ go, home, hoping, road,
                clothes, grow, below
Group C: /ʌ/ son, among, mother
Group D: /aʊ/ now, brown, house,
                mountain

2 **How do you say these words? Mark them A, B, C or D. Then listen to the tape.**

alone		sorry
cottage		boat
know		bottle
another		town
love		broken
about		month

3 You will hear four sentences. Cover this page, and write them down.

DICTATION

You will hear two of the texts from *Houses* (Classroom Book, page 38).

Listen and write down what you hear.

WRITING SKILLS: Joining ideas

1 Look at these examples.

His flat is on the fifth floor. It's got a balcony.
His flat is on the fifth floor **and** it's got a balcony.

Their house is very big. It's only got a small garden.
Their house is very big **but** it's only got a small garden.

My flat is on a main road. It's rather noisy.
My flat is on a main road **so** it's rather noisy.

2 Fill the gaps with *and, but* or *so*.

a Our flat is very old .... it's in good
condition.
b My flat is near the town centre .... it's
very convenient for the shops.
c Her cottage is very comfortable .... it's
rather damp in winter.
d He lives near an underground station ....
it doesn't take long to get into the centre.
e My flat faces south .... it has a big
balcony.

**3 Paragraphs A and B say the same thing, but one
paragraph presents the ideas in a more natural way.
Which one?**

A I'm quite pleased with my new flat. It has three
bedrooms and a large kitchen. It's near the city
centre, so it's very convenient for my work.
Unfortunately, it's on the ground floor, so it's a
bit dark.

B I'm quite pleased with my new flat. It has a large
kitchen. It's near the city centre and it has three
bedrooms. Unfortunately, it's on the ground floor,
so it's a bit dark. It's very convenient for my work.

**4 Join these ideas together to make a paragraph.
Use *and, but* or *so* where necessary.**

It's not too
noisy.

It has a living room,
a bedroom and a
small kitchen.

It has beautiful
views across the
bay.

It's near the town
centre.

It's near the
beach.

I've just
moved
to a new
flat.

It's a long way
from the main
road.

....
....
....
....
....
....
....
....
....
....
....

9 Quantity

A A, some & any

Fill the gaps with *a(n)*, *some* or *any*.

1 Yesterday I wanted spaghetti bolognese for my dinner. I bought .... meat at the butcher, and got .... tomatoes at the supermarket. Then I remembered that I didn't have .... cheese, so I bought .... nice big piece, and went home – and found that there wasn't .... spaghetti. So I had .... cheese sandwich instead.

2 I was on a train in Germany, and I saw a man with .... bucket of flour standing by an open window. As I watched he took .... flour and threw it out of the window. Then he threw .... more.
'Why are you doing that?' I asked.
'To keep the elephants away,' he replied.
'But there aren't .... elephants in Germany,' I said.
'You see – ' he said, 'it works!'

> **a, some or any**
>
> **a:**
> He's got **a** bike but he hasn't got **a** car.
>
> **some:**
> We drank **some** coffee and ate **some** biscuits.
>
> **any:**
> Have you got **any** money? There isn't **any** food in the house. And I haven't got **any** cigarettes.

B Quantity expressions

The sentences below aren't true. Rewrite them with different quantity expressions.
Examples:

Millipedes have*n't* got *many* legs. → *Millipedes have got a lot of legs.*
There are*n't many* icebergs in Singapore. → *There aren't any icebergs in Singapore.*

1 There's *a lot of* rain in the Sahara Desert.

....

2 Howard Hughes did*n't* have *much* money.

....

3 *Quite a lot of* countries have nuclear weapons.

....

4 Nurses earn *a lot of* money.

....

5 *Not many* people speak Spanish.

....

6 The Americans did*n't* find *much* gold on the moon.

....

C How much...? & How many...?

Rewrite these questions using *How much...?* or *How many...?*

Examples:

Have we got a packet of rice? half a packet? → *How much rice have we got?*

Are there 15 ounces in a pound? 16? 20? → *How many ounces are there in a pound?*

1 Does he smoke five cigarettes a day? 20? more than 20?

....

2 Is there a lot of petrol in the car? or not much?

....

3 Do you want a glass of milk? a litre?

....

4 Were there ten people at the meeting? 20? more than 20?

....

5 Does she earn $200 a week? $400? $600?

....

6 Are there 720 minutes in a day? 1,440? 3600?

....

7 Did they buy one bottle of wine? two bottles? three?

....

D Too & enough

People often complain about where they live. Make complaints from the table.

1 *There are too many cars.*

2 ....

....

....

3 ....

....

There	's too much are too many	cars things to do in the evening fresh air burglaries
	isn't enough aren't enough	rubbish in the streets public telephones noise from traffic

4 ....

5 ....

6 ....

7 ....

Now write three real complaints about your own town.

8 ....

9 ....

10 ....

TRANSLATION

Translate into your own language:

1 – Could you lend me some money?
  – I'm afraid I haven't got any.

....

....

2 – How much food do we need?
  – I don't know. How many people
    are coming?

....

....

....

3 She meets quite a lot of foreigners.

....

4 There are too many cars and there
  aren't enough places to park.

....

....

Now cover up the left-hand side, and translate your sentences back into English.

LISTENING: Panel discussion

You will hear part of a panel discussion about news programmes on television.

1 Listen to the presenter's introduction and complete her questions:

We're going to ask our guests for their opinions about

news programmes. Are they ....? Do you

think there are .... or

...................................? Do the current ....

focus on ....?

2 Now listen to the three replies. Which sentences are closest to the opinions of the three speakers? Write *1, 2, 3* or – .

.... *a* News programmes should focus on local news, not international news.

.... *b* News programmes focus on just the right things.

.... *c* News programmes aren't serious enough.

.... *d* There should be more international news and less local news.

.... *e* There should be more news programmes.

3 What do the speakers say about these things?

Speaker 1: wars and famines

....

Speaker 2: 24-hour news programmes

....

Speaker 3: disasters

....

PRONUNCIATION: Secondary stress

1 Listen to these sentences. Notice that:

– each sentence has one main stress.
  (e.g. holidays)

– other words are also stressed.
  (e.g. Where, going)

Where are you going for your **ho**lidays?

How many **chil**dren have you got?

A box of **ma**tches, please.

Did you see the **game** last Friday?

Hondas are made in Ja**pan**.

2 Look at these sentences. How do you think they are said? Mark the *main stress* and *secondary stresses*.

a Give me a kiss.
b Let me see it.
c She missed her plane.
d It's time to go to bed.
e How many languages do you speak?
f They usually have lunch at work.
g What are you doing on Monday?

Now listen and check your answers. Then practise saying the sentences.

DICTATION

You will hear five of the opinions in *Points of view* (Classroom Book, page 44).

Listen and write down what you hear.

READING: Money

For a magazine article, five people answered these two questions:

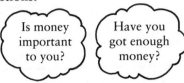

Is money important to you?

Have you got enough money?

What can you tell about them? Complete the table below. Write ✔ (= Yes), ✗ (= No) or ? (= Can't tell).

Steve, 24, economist

Yes, I think money is important. One day I want to buy my own house, and I'll want my family to have a good standard of living. Some people worry too much about money. They work all the time because they want lots and lots of it, and they don't see enough of their family and friends. I like money, but I don't worry about it. I just earn enough for my needs, and I have lots of free time too.

Josephine, 75, retired teacher

Money is important to me as a safety net. If the car goes wrong, or the cat falls ill, or the house needs repairing, it's good to know I can get help immediately without worrying about the cost. I don't smoke or drink, and I don't go on expensive holidays, so I can live quite happily on my pension. I don't want to be rich – but if someone offers me a million dollars, I certainly won't say 'No'.

Tony, 52, company director

Every morning when I open the post I look first to see if there are any cheques. I always pay cheques into the bank straight away. Then I look to see if there are any bills. If there are – and there always are – I put them away with the others, and pay them later – much later. Money's a strange thing – there's never enough of it, is there? This may sound boring, but I think making money is fun.

Larissa, 17, student

I need money but I don't like it. I would rather make leather sandals and exchange them for watermelons at market, or something like that. Money is OK if you've got a lot of it, but it causes terrible problems for people who haven't got any. Have I got enough money? Yes, I think so.

Brian, 29, builder

Money's important to me because I have to keep up the payments on my house and pay off my bank loan. But I'd rather have less money and fewer bills – and fewer worries. I don't enjoy working – I only do it because I don't have enough money. If I didn't have to earn money, I would stop work and spend my time taking photographs and rebuilding old cars.

	Steve	Josephine	Tony	Larissa	Brian
1 Who thinks money is important?	✔				
2 Who has a job?				?	
3 Who owns his/her own house?				✗	
4 Who likes money?		?			
5 Who thinks he/she has enough money?					

10 Clothes

A They come in pairs

All the answers come in pairs. Write in the answers, and you'll find another pair, going down.

Things worn on the legs and feet usually come in pairs. For example, I usually wear a pair of (3) to work, but often change into a pair of blue (6) when I get home – or even a pair of (4) if the weather's very hot. On my feet I wear a pair of black (1) over a pair of short (8), although in hot weather I prefer a pair of open-toed (2).

My sister doesn't wear (8) very often – she usually wears a pair of (7). And my mother prefers an old-fashioned pair of (5).

But it's not only on the legs and feet that things come in pairs. Both my sister and my mother often wear a pair of (9).

B On and off

Fill the gaps with a verb from the box, in the right form. You'll have to use some verbs more than once.

take off	get dressed
wear	get undressed
put on	get changed
try on	

1 'Do you want me to ....?' he asked.

'No, not completely,' replied the doctor. 'Just .... your shirt, please, so that I can examine you.'

2 After her bath, she .... and went downstairs. It was a bit cold, so before she left the house she .... her coat.

3 The first time I .... the jacket .... it seemed a bit small. But the shop assistant reminded me that I was .... a thick sweater. So I .... the sweater, and the jacket felt much more comfortable.

4 I can't .... these old jeans to the theatre. I'd better .... I won't be long.

5 He was very tired when he got home. He .... his coat, threw it on a chair, ... and went to bed.

C Materials and patterns

What have you got that's made of cotton, wool, and leather?
For each material, write about two things.

a made of cotton
  Example: *a green and white striped shirt.*

1 ....

2 ....

b made of wool
  Example: *some gloves with a red check pattern*

3 ....

4 ....

c made of leather
  Example: *a pair of plain red shoes*

5 ....

6 ....

New words

Use this space to write down new words from the unit, with your own notes and examples.

....

....

....

....

....

....

....

....

....

....

....

....

....

....

TRANSLATION

Translate into your own language:

1 You can't miss him. He's wearing a white jacket, and he's carrying a striped umbrella.

....
....
....

2 Get dressed quickly – there's someone at the door.

....
....

3 I like your pullover. It suits you.

....

4 – Do those shoes fit you?
– No, they're a bit small for me.

....
....

Now cover up the left-hand side, and translate your sentences back into English.

LISTENING: Working clothes

1 You will hear four people saying what clothes they wear to work. Listen and complete the table.

	Which picture?	What clothes does the speaker mention?
1		
2		
3		
4		

2 What do you know about each person's work?

1 ....

2 ....

3 ....

4 ....

SOUND AND SPELLING: Words with *o* (2)

1 Listen to these words on the tape.
   Group A: /ɔː/ more, shore, born, door, four
   Group B: /ʊ/ good, cook, woollen, should
   Group C: /uː/ food, too, boots, two, shoes
   Group D: /ɔɪ/ boy, annoyed, noise, join

2 How do you say these words? Mark them A, B, C or D. Then listen to the tape.

	voice		enjoy
	food		wood
	before		floor
	course		loose
	look		lose
	choose		foot

3 You will hear four sentences. Cover this page, and write them down.

DICTATION

You will hear most of the dialogue from *Clothes quiz* (Classroom Book, page 47 and page 126).

Listen and write down what you hear.

WRITING SKILLS: Sequence (1)

My next-door neighbour is a person of very regular habits. He always leaves home at exactly nine in the morning. First he goes to the newsagent's and buys the morning paper. Then he goes to a café (always the same one), orders a cup of black coffee and reads his paper. After that he goes for a walk once round the park, and then he goes home.

1 These expressions are used for showing sequence. Find them in the text.

> then
> and then
> after that
> and
> first

Which are used

a to begin a new sentence? ....

b to join sentences together? ....

2 Join these sentences together to complete the paragraph. Use expressions from the box.

I collect the children from school.
I take them to the park.
We come home.
We have supper together.
I play with them for an hour.
They have a bath.
They get ready for bed.
I read them a story.
I can sit down and relax.

Don't ever try to phone me between three o'clock and seven o'clock, ...

because I'm always busy. ....

....

....

....

....

....

....

3 Are there any times in your day when you have a regular routine? Write about them.

....

....

....

....

....

....

....

11 Future plans

A New Year Resolutions: going to

Read the text, and complete Ebenezer's New Year Resolutions. Use *going to* and *not going to*.

It was New Year's Eve. Ebenezer sat alone at home. 'Where is everyone?' he wondered. 'Why am I alone?'

'Do you really want to know?' said a voice behind his chair.

'Wh- Who's that?' cried Ebenezer.

'I am the Ghost of the New Year,' said the voice, 'and I'm going to tell you why you're alone. Well, to start with, you aren't a very nice person. You shout at everyone. You don't smile. You never take your family out. You don't visit your friends. You spend all your money on yourself – when did you last give your children a present? And you have some very bad habits. You get drunk. You watch too much TV. You don't often have a bath. You only shave once a week. And another thing. You don't ...'

'All right! All right!' said Ebenezer. 'That's enough. I understand.' And he took a pen and started to write some New Year Resolutions ...

I'm going to be a nice person.
....

I'm not going to shout at people.
....

I'm going
....

....

....

....

....

....

....

....

....

....

....

B Times and arrangements

Use the *Present continuous* and the time expressions in the box to describe Ebenezer's arrangements.

this (morning)	**on** (Monday)
tomorrow (morning)	**in** (three weeks)
next (Tuesday, week)	

It was Monday 1st May when the ghost came again. 'How are you?' he asked.

'Terrible!' said Ebenezer sadly. 'I haven't got any time for myself! Look. This afternoon ...' And he showed the ghost these entries in his diary:

May 1st	3.00	Take children swimming
	8.00	Browns come to dinner
May 2nd	9.00	To hairdresser's
	7.30	School concert
May 3rd		Have lunch with in-laws
May 5th		Daughter's birthday party
May 8–12		Brother & family to stay
July 1–15		Family holiday at seaside

This afternoon he's taking the children swimming.

....

....

....

....

....

....

....

....

....

....

....

....

....

C (I expect) I'll (probably)

What are your plans for the rest of today? Write them down. If you're sure, use *going to* or the *Present continuous*. If you're not sure, use *I'll probably* or *I expect I'll*.

Examples:

I'm collecting the children from school at 3.30.
I'll probably do some washing tonight.
I expect I'll watch a film on TV.
I'll probably go to bed at about midnight.

1 ....

2 ....

3 ....

4 ....

5 ....

TRANSLATION

Translate into your own language:

1 When I leave college, I'm going to get a job abroad.

....
....

2 – What are you doing on Friday evening?
   – I don't know yet. I'll probably just stay at home.

....
....
....

3 I'm taking my exams in two weeks.

....

4 When are you getting married?

....

Now cover up the left-hand side, and translate your sentences back into English.

LISTENING: Two journeys

You will hear two people talking about their plans for a trip around Europe.

1 Which places are they going to visit? Fill the gaps with places from the box.

South of France	Rome	Florence	Pisa
Barcelona	Venice	London	Paris

Journey A

1 London
2 ....
3 ....
4 ....
5 ....
6 ....
7 London

Journey B

1 London
2 ....
3 ....
4 ....
5 London

2 How are the people going to travel? Complete the table.

	Journey A	Journey B
ferry		
train		
hitch-hike		
plane	*Venice–London*	–
car		

PRONUNCIATION: Rhythm

1 We say unstressed syllables more quickly than stressed syllables. Listen to the rhythm of these sentences.

Go			home.
Stay	at		home.
Go	to	the	shops.
He	**went**	to the	shops.
He's	**go**ing	to the	shops.

2 What rhythm do you think these sentences have? Mark the stressed syllables, and say them aloud.

a Go away.
b There's a fly in my soup.
c They arrived very late.
d How do you do?
e We're meeting some friends for a drink.
f I don't like cats.
g Are you reading that newspaper?

Now listen and check your answers. Then practise saying the sentences.

DICTATION

You will hear two of the texts from *Intentions* (Classroom Book, page 50).

Listen and write down what you hear.

READING: Letters

Here are parts of three letters in which people talk about their plans for the following week. What can you tell about each person? Answer the questions by writing V, B and/or A.

1 Who's got a busy week ahead? ....V, B, A........

2 Who has children? ....

3 Who's going to have visitors? ....

4 Who's going on a journey? ....

5 Who has definite plans for the weekend? ....

6 Who drives a car? ....

7 Who has a job? ....

8 Who's going to have the most enjoyable week? ....

Valerie

Tomorrow I'm going strawberry picking, and Ingrid and Tony are coming round for the evening. Tuesday's going to be shopping and ironing, then shopping and ironing, and then some more ironing. Wednesday is Emma's school sports day — I wonder if she'll come last in everything again. The in-laws are coming to stay for a couple of weeks on Sunday, so I think I'm going to be kept quite busy at the end of the week getting myself organised for their arrival. But on Saturday evening, at least, I won't be doing the washing-up: I'm going out for a meal with some friends from the office.

Brigitte

What a week! On Thursday I'm going to Nottingham for a book exhibition, then further north to Gateshead on Friday evening for this year's Festival of Languages, which will be held there on Saturday. Then back to London on Sunday, and hope that I won't get stuck in traffic on the motorway. Next week it'll be work as usual. Most evenings I'll be visiting Paul's mother in hospital. She's been there for over a week now, and it looks as if she's going to stay quite a bit longer. This means a lot of rushing around. I just hope that the summer will be less strenuous than these last few months. Perhaps I'll find the time at last to do all those things I really want to do. And who knows — perhaps I'll even manage to come to Edinburgh to see you all!

Alan

Dad's staying with us at the moment, which is great because Paula and David have finished school for the summer. He's leaving tomorrow, and so this evening we're all going to go out for a meal together. On Wednesday I'm going to Paris for two days, to give a lecture. If I have time, I'll probably try to visit the Gauguin exhibition you mentioned, but I should think I'll be too busy. We haven't got any special plans for the weekend. If the weather's good we'll probably all drive out to the country and have a picnic. Otherwise I'll probably try and catch up with some work. But if you have any better ideas, I'm open to suggestion!

12 How do you feel?

A What's wrong?

Write the missing words in the diagrams.

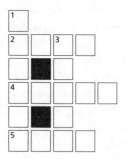
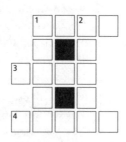
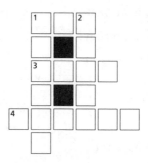

– What's the (1▼) ? Have you got a head (2▶) ?
– Yes, I have. And my back (3▼) , too. I'm probably just a bit (4▶).
– Well, why don't you lie down and have a (5▶)?

I never (1▼) cigarettes. They always make me feel (1▶). Besides that, they give you a (3▶) throat, and they make your (4▶) yellow. And after a time you start getting pains in your (2▼) …

– (1▶) do you feel?
– Not very well. I've got a nasty (3▶) in my (2▼).
– Oh dear. How did it (1▼)?
– I, think I did too much typing yesterday.
– Well, I hope it gets (4▶) soon.

B Good advice

Give two pieces of good advice for each of the following.
Example: 'My legs really hurt after that long walk.'
Have a nice hot bath.
Sit down and put your feet up.

1 'I can't get to sleep.'

....

....

2 'I've got toothache.'

....

....

3 'I need to lose some weight.'

....

....

4 'I've got a sore throat.'

....

....

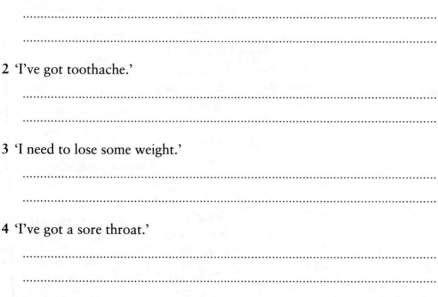

C Phrases

Complete these sentences with a suitable phrase. Each answer should include one item from box A and one item from box B.

A	B
~~ask~~	appointment
examine	bed
give	chemist's
go	chest
have	pills
make	prescription
stay	~~questions~~
take	toothache

Example:

The doctor *asked me a lot of questions* about myself and my family.

1 'I'd like to .... to see the doctor, please.'

2 If ...., you should go and see a dentist straight away.

3 'Take off your shirt, please,' said the doctor. 'I need to ....'

4 'You must .... every four hours.'

5 Before I left, the doctor .... for some medicine.

6 'I want you to .... for a day or two and get some rest.'

7 'Would you .... and get my medicine for me?'

New words

Use this space to write down new words from the unit, with your own notes and examples.

....

....

....

....

....

....

....

....

....

....

....

....

....

....

TRANSLATION

Translate into your own language:

1 – What's the matter with you?
   – I feel terrible. I think I've got 'flu.

   ....

   ....

2 I won't have any cake, thanks. I'm
   on a diet.

   ....

   ....

3 Could I make an appointment to
   see the dentist, please?

   ....

   ....

4 – How do you feel now?
   – Much better, thanks.

   ....

Now cover up the left-hand side, and translate your sentences back into English.

LISTENING: Feeling ill

You will hear a man talking about a time when he was ill.
Listen and answer the questions.

1 Find *seven* factual differences between the text and the
   story on the tape.

   I was sitting at home one day watching television when
   I suddenly started feeling ill. I felt very cold and my
   throat hurt. I went to see the doctor, and he asked me
   questions and examined my ears and throat. He told
   me I had 'flu, gave me a prescription for some medicine
   and told me to stay in bed for a week. I did what he
   said, and only two days later I felt better.

   a ....

   b ....

   c ....

   d ....

   e ....

   f ....

   g ....

2 *a* What does the man think was wrong with him?

   ....

   b Why does he think he got better?

   ....

SOUND AND SPELLING: Words with *u*

1 Listen to these words on the tape.
   Group A: /ʌ/ bus, supper, jumper, under
   Group B: /uː/ blue, usually, supermarket,
   suit
   Group C: /ɜː/ nurse, Thursday, church, burn
   Group D: /ʊ/ full, pudding, put, butcher

2 How do you say these words? Mark them
   A, B, C or D. Then listen to the tape.

☐	pull	☐	push
☐	Sunday	☐	uniform
☐	running	☐	sugar
☐	curtains	☐	hurt
☐	fruit	☐	include
☐	student	☐	hungry

3 You will hear four sentences. Cover this
   page, and write them down.

DICTATION

You will hear part of the reading text from *All
in the mind* (Classroom Book, page 57).
Listen and write down what you hear.

WRITING SKILLS: Listing

1 Look at these sentences:

> Eva had a terrible cold.
> 1 She had a headache.
> 2 Her throat was sore.
> 3 She couldn't stop sneezing.

We can join the ideas together like this:

A Eva had a terrible cold. She had a headache, her throat was sore and she couldn't stop sneezing.

B Eva had a terrible cold. She had a headache and her throat was sore. Also, she couldn't stop sneezing.

2 Punctuate these sentences:

a I really enjoyed the party the food was delicious there was lots of good music and I met some very interesting people

b I don't like my flat-mate much she never cleans the flat and she plays loud music all the time also she has some very strange friends.

....
....
....
....
....
....

3 Add some ideas to these sentences. Use expressions from the box.

a It's not worth going into the city centre on a Saturday. ...

b That dress looks really good on you. ...

c After 20 miles, she knew she couldn't walk any further. ...

d It's a very good restaurant. ...

> It's very clean.
> There's nowhere to park.
> It's a very unusual colour.
> The food's always freshly cooked.
> Her legs ached.
> It's terribly crowded everywhere.
> She felt tired and hungry.
> It goes with your eyes.
> There are long traffic jams.
> The prices are quite reasonable.
> It's just the right length.
> Her feet were sore.

a ....
....
....
....

b ....
....
....
....

c ....
....
....

d ....
....
....
....

Revision and extension

1 Verb forms

Write the correct form of the verbs.
Example:
They *got* (get) married yesterday.

1 He .... (send) me a letter a week
ago, but it .... (*not – arrive*) until
yesterday.
2 Some friends .... (come) round
tomorrow evening and we .... (go)
to the theatre together.
3 She usually .... (drive) everywhere,
but last week her car .... (break)
down, so at the moment she ....
(*not – go*) out much.
4 Two months ago they .... (sell) their
car and .... (buy) two bicycles.
5 When I .... (be) young, there
.... (*not – be*) many cars on the
roads.

2 Asking questions

Complete the questions.
Example:
What *are you going to do* tonight?
I'm going to watch an old movie on TV.

1 – Why .... your job?
– It was boring and I didn't get enough money.
2 – How many states .... in the USA?
– Um, 51, I think.
3 – .... any money?
– No, I haven't, I'm afraid.
4 – Hello. When ....
– Just a minute ago. We just came through the
door.
5 – .... any butter?
– Yes, there's some in the fridge.
6 – What .... to drink?
– Just some mineral water, please.
7 – How much ....?
– Only $20. Why don't you try it on?

3 Prepositions

Fill the gaps with
prepositions from the
box.

on	at	to
with	of	in

1 I'm sorry. I'm busy
.... the weekend, so I'll see you ....
Wednesday instead.
2 I expect I'll be back .... about a month.
3 They've just moved .... a new flat ....
the suburbs.
4 I bought this necklace to go .... my blue dress.
5 Their flat's .... the 10th floor, so they've got a
wonderful view .... the river.
6 They got married .... 16th March.

4 Quantity expressions

Fill the gaps with
expressions from the
box.

some	any	enough
much	many	a lot of

1 Your trouble is, you watch too ....
television, you go to too .... parties, and
you don't get .... sleep.
2 – Have you got .... 10p pieces? I want to
make .... phone calls.
– How .... do you want?
– Oh, three will be ....
3 I'm very happy really. I've got .... friends,
and .... money to live comfortably. And I
haven't got .... worries at all.

5 Word order

Put these jumbled sentences in the right order. Remember to begin each
sentence with a capital letter.

Example: tomorrow after leaving the we're day .
        We're leaving the day after tomorrow.

1 the made he doctor appointment an see to .

....

2 probably tonight a for we'll out meal go .

....

3 gold wearing of pair she's earrings a .

....

4 left half he an home ago hour .

....

5 a kilo much jam is in sugar there of how ?

....

6 afternoon was baby the Friday born on .

....

6 Writing paragraphs

Write a short paragraph (2 or 3 sentences) on the following:

1 Describe the room that you're in now.

....

....

....

2 Are you a healthy person? What do you do that's good/bad for you?

....

....

....

3 Is your country hot or cold? What do people wear when they are out of doors?

....

....

....

4 Where are you going for your next holiday?

....

....

13 Comparison

A Comparative and superlative

Complete the table with comparative and superlative forms.

Adjective	Comparative	Superlative
clean	cleaner	cleanest
small		
fat		
wide		
heavy		
careful		
exciting		
intelligent		
good		
bad		
far		
much/many		

Comparative and superlative forms

One-syllable adjectives:
   cold – **colder** – **coldest**
   big – **bigger** – **biggest**

Two-syllable adjectives:
   ending in y:
   friendly – **friendlier** – **friendliest**
   most others:
   boring – **more boring** – **most boring**
   helpful – **more helpful** – **most helpful**

Three or more syllables:
   popular – **more popular** – **most popular**
   interesting – **more interesting** – **most interesting**

Irregular adjectives:
   good, bad, far, much/many

B Opposites

Rewrite each sentence using an opposite adjective.
The *first letters* of the adjectives in numbers 1–6 give the missing word in 7.

Example:

Geckos are *smaller* than crocodiles. → Crocodiles *are bigger than geckos.*

1 Gold is *more expensive* than silver.

   Silver ....

2 Lambs are *younger* than sheep.

   Sheep ....

3 Steel is *heavier* than aluminium.

   Aluminium ....

4 California is *wetter* than Arizona.

   Arizona ....

5 Listening is *more difficult* than reading.

   Reading ....

6 The Third World is *poorer* than the West.

   The West ....

7 Mars is ☐ ☐ ☐ ☐ ☐ ☐ than Venus.

C World records

What world records can you find in the box? Some words are used more than once; some are not used.

Examples:

The Vatican is the smallest country in the world.
China has got the largest population in the world.

The Vatican	rich	population
China	high	caviare
The USSR	good	mountain
The whale	small	place
The cheetah	expensive	river
The Nile	sunny	fish
M.Everest	large	country
The Sahara	fast	mammal
Beluga	long	animal

1 ....

2 ....

3 ....

4 ....

5 ....

6 ....

7 ....

D People

Who's the most boring person you know?
Why is he/she boring?
Write about four people you know.

Example:

The most boring person I know is my younger brother. He just watches television all the time.

1 boring

....

....

....

2 intelligent

....

....

....

3 interesting

....

....

....

4 unusual

....

....

....

TRANSLATION

Translate into your own language:

1 I think she's the most intelligent person I've ever met.

....

....

2 – What's the best way to get there?
  – Well, the bus is cheaper, but it's more comfortable by train.

....

....

....

3 – This is a good restaurant, isn't it?
  – I prefer Bruno's myself. I think the food's much better there.

....

....

....

Now cover up the left-hand side, and translate your sentences back into English.

LISTENING: The most and the least

You will hear three people (A, B, C) talking about the musical instruments they play, the languages they speak, and the countries they have visited.

1 Which person:

   a is the most musical? ....

   b is the least musical? ....

   c speaks the most languages? ....

   d speaks the fewest languages? ....

   e has visited the most countries? ....

   f has visited the fewest countries? ....

2 Listen again and answer these questions.

   a Which of the people still play(s) the piano? ....

   b Which of the people could make themselves understood in:
      – Switzerland? ....
      – Mexico? ....
      – Japan? ....

   c Which speakers do you think have been to:
      – Switzerland? ....
      – Mexico? ....
      – Japan? ....

PRONUNCIATION: Reduced vowels (3)

1 Listen to the words in the box. They have a full sound when they are stressed, but have the sound /ə/ when they are unstressed.

are	Are you there? What are you doing?
can	Can you swim? Yes, I can. I think I can see them.
was	He wasn't at home. No, but I was. There was plenty of food.

2 Listen to these sentences. Is the word pronounced (1) with a full sound? (2) with the sound /ə/? Write 1 or 2.

   a does ....   g does ....

   b are ....   h were ....

   c was ....   i was ....

   d do ....   j are ....

   e does ....   k were ....

   f can ....   l was ....

   Now listen again, and practise saying the sentences.

DICTATION

You will hear four of the texts from *Outstanding features* (Classroom Book, page 61). Listen and write down what you hear.

READING: Four planets

What do you know about the Solar System?
Mark these statements T (True) or F (False).
Then check your answers in the text.

1 A year on Pluto is more than 100 years on Earth.

2 Mercury is the nearest planet to the Sun.

3 The biggest hurricane in the Solar System is on Jupiter.

4 Mercury is the hottest planet.

5 Jupiter is bigger than all the other planets put together.

6 Mercury is heavier than Pluto.

7 The diameter of the Sun is more than 20 times bigger than the diameter of Jupiter.

8 Uranus is the furthest planet from Earth.

9 Earth's atmosphere is thinner than Venus's atmosphere.

10 Pluto is the smallest of the planets.

11 Venus is the easiest planet to see from Earth.

Mercury

Mercury is the closest planet to the Sun. Because of this, it has scorching daytime temperatures of up to 350°C. This is over seven times hotter than the hottest temperature ever recorded on Earth: 57.7°C at Azizia, Libya, in 1922.

At night, the temperature can drop to –170°C because there is no atmosphere to trap the heat. This is more than seven times colder than the temperature inside the freezer compartment of a refrigerator.

Jupiter

Jupiter is the largest planet in our Solar System. It is more than 1,300 times bigger than Earth, and bigger than all the other planets put together. But it is still much smaller than the Sun: if the Sun was the size of a tennis ball 8 cm in diameter, Jupiter would be the size of a pea 0.85 cm in diameter.

There is a reddish patch on Jupiter, known as the Great Red Spot. This is the biggest hurricane in the Solar System, with swirling clouds about 38,500 km long by 11,000 km wide. It is as big as three Earths.

Venus

Seen from Earth, Venus is by far the brightest of the planets. It is often called the "evening star". Although Venus and Earth are about the same size, their atmospheres are completely different. Venus's atmosphere is so thick that at the planet's surface the pressure is 90 times that on Earth. This thick atmosphere traps the Sun's heat rather like a greenhouse, so that the temperature reaches about 500°C.

Pluto

Pluto was discovered in 1930. With a diameter of 2,400 km, it is smaller than our Moon, making it the smallest and lightest planet in the Solar System.

For most of the time, Pluto is the furthest planet from Earth (sometimes Neptune is the furthest). An aeroplane travelling at a speed of 1,000 kph would take about 670 years to travel from Earth to Pluto.

A person on Pluto would never live for one Pluto year. The Pluto year is the time it takes Pluto to travel once round the Sun – about 147 years.

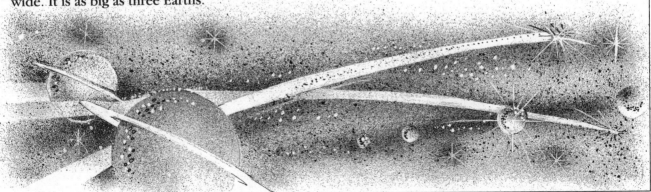

Adapted from *The Usborne Book of Space Facts*

14 About town

A Guests

Here are some guests you're expecting over the next few months. Write down some things that you'll do with them.

Has lots of money ... loves good food ... gets up at 11.30 ... lazy ... a night person
Take him to an expensive restaurant for dinner.
....

....

Cultured ... not very active ... doesn't go out after dark

....

....

Like doing and watching sports ... enjoy watching films ... interested in animals

....

....

Love shopping ... enjoy taking photographs ... good dancers

....

....

B Giving directions

Complete the conversations using expressions from the box.

Example:

A Excuse me, can you tell me the way to the Post Office?
B *Yes. You go straight along this road. Go over the river, and then turn right at the cinema. You'll see it on the left.*

A Excuse me, how do I get to the university?
B ....
....

A Excuse me, can you tell me the way to the swimming pool?
B ....
....

A Excuse me, ...
B ....
....

Turn	left right	(at ...)
Go straight on		

Go	under over past	...

You'll see it It's	on the	left. right.

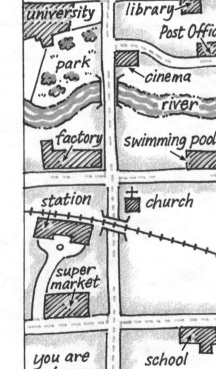

C Describing towns

Continue these descriptions of towns.

Examples:

It's a rather dirty town ... *There's a lot of traffic, and the streets are full of litter.*

It's a good place for old people to live ... *It's got a pleasant climate, there isn't much traffic, and there are lots of parks.*

1 It's a good place for students ... .

....

....

2 It's a very beautiful town ... .

....

....

3 It's a really boring place to live ... .

....

....

4 It's a good place to live if you've got young children ... .

....

....

New words

Use this space to write down new words from the unit, with your own notes and examples.

....

....

....

....

....

....

....

....

....

....

....

....

TRANSLATION

Translate into your own language:

1 – Excuse me. Is there a department
    store anywhere near here?
   – Yes, there's one just along the road.

....

....

....

2 There's a very good sports centre
  with a swimming pool, tennis courts
  and a football pitch.

....

....

....

3 There aren't many places to go in the
  evenings.

....

....

Now cover up the left-hand side, and translate your sentences back into English.

LISTENING: Living in London

You will hear a man and a woman talking about living in London.

1 Listen and complete the table.
  Which things does the man talk about? Which does the woman talk about? (Write M or W.)
  Do they think these are good or bad points? (Write *Good* or *Bad*.)

		M/W	Good/Bad
a	going to work		
b	going out in the evening		
c	noise		
d	people's behaviour		
e	food shops		
f	the city's atmosphere		

2 What do they say about each topic in the table above? Write a brief comment for each one.

  a *The underground's always crowded.* ....

  b ....

  c ....

  d ....

  e ....

  f ....

SOUNDS AND SPELLING: Words with *y*

1 Listen to these words on the tape.
  Group A: /i/ city, slowly, happy, angry
  Group B: /aɪ/ my, cry, why, flying

2 How do you say these words? Mark them A or B. Then listen to the tape.

	dry		typist
	carry		hungry
	friendly		trying

3 Sometimes, *y* changes to *ie*. For example:

  try – tries – tried; carry – carries – carried
  city – cities; happy – happier
  but: play – plays – played; boy – boys

  You will hear sentences containing forms of these words. Write down the words.

  a marry   c easy   e party
  b cry   d enjoy   f stay

4 You will hear four sentences. Cover this page, and write them down.

DICTATION

You will hear one of the texts from *Los Angeles* (Classroom Book, page 67).

Listen and write down what you hear.

WRITING SKILLS: Reason and contrast

1 Look at these examples.

It's a very beautiful old city, **so** it's always full of tourists in summer.

As
Because | it's a very beautiful old city, it's always full of tourists in summer.

It's a very beautiful town to look at, **but** there isn't much to do there.
Although it's a very beautiful town to look at, there isn't much to do there.

2 Fill the gaps with *so, as, because, but* or *although*.

a .... there aren't many good restaurants, there are plenty of cheap cafés.

b .... it's a large sea port, it has a cosmopolitan atmosphere and there's always a lot going on.

c There's a large theatre, ... they don't perform very interesting plays .... I don't go there very often.

d The river's very polluted .... it's not a good idea to swim in it, ... there's a very good swimming pool.

3 Join these ideas using words from the box. Change the order of the ideas if you like.

and	so
but	although
as	because

a It's a small town.
  It's easy to get to know people.
  People are very friendly.

....
....

b There are factories all round the town.
  The air's very polluted.
  It's a very unhealthy place to live.

....
....
....

c It's a large industrial town.
  It's quite ugly.
  I like living there.
  It has a very friendly atmosphere.

....
....
....

d It's only a small town.
  It's very lively.
  There's lots to do in the evenings.
  It's by the sea.
  It's very popular with tourists.

....
....
....

15 Past and present

A Irregular squares

All the answers are past participles. They are all irregular verbs.

1 ▶ She has .... school now. She's at college. (4)

1 ▼ I've .... my coat. I can't find it anywhere. (4)

2 ▼ Ah, there it is. It's OK – I've .... it! (5)

3 ▶ Have you ever .... in the Black Sea? (4)

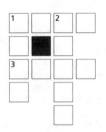

1 ▼ I've never .... in a tent before. (5)

2 ▶ I've .... across the Atlantic but I've never sailed. (5)

3 ▼ We've ....! We're the champions! (3)

4 ▶ Oh dear. I've .... too much money this week. (5)

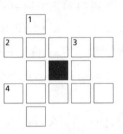

1 ▼ They've just .... a new video recorder. (6)

2 ▶ Have you .... your bike yet? I'd like to buy it. (4)

3 ▼ Hey – you haven't .... the washing up yet. (4)

4 ▶ Tony's not here. He's .... to a meeting. (4)

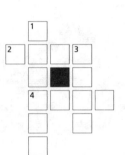

1 ▼ I've paid two bills and .... three letters. (7)

2 ▶ He's .... a lot taller recently (5)

3 ▼ She's not asleep – she's just .... up. (5)

4 ▶ I've .... two aspirin, but my head still hurts. (5)

5 ▶ Have you ever .... to Shanghai? (4)

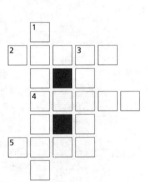

B Not ... yet

What hasn't happened yet? Rewrite each sentence using a verb from the box with *not ... yet*.

Example:

They're still here.
They haven't gone yet.

| arrive |
| come back |
| find |
| get up |
| give up |
| go |
| leave |

1 She's still looking for a flat.

....

2 They're still out.

....

3 He's still in bed.

....

4 We still smoke.

....

5 They're still waiting for the bus.

....

6 I'm still studying at university.

....

C Personal news

Imagine that you've just done three of these things:

- bought something   – changed jobs   – been ill   – been on holiday
- moved house   – met someone   – lost something   – broken up with a boyfriend/girlfriend

Write your news as part of a letter.

Examples:

*I've been ill in bed this week. I had the 'flu, and I had to stay in bed,
but I'm better now.*

*I'm afraid I've lost Helen's address. I can't find it anywhere. I'll ask her
sister when I see her.*

1 ....
....
....
2 ....
....
....
3 ....
....
....

D Questions of experience

Here are some answers. What were the questions?
Write a question with *Have you ever...?* for each.

1 Q: *Have you ever flown in a helicopter?* ....

   A: Only once. It was very frightening.

2 Q: ....

   A: No, never. But most of my friends have.

3 Q: ....

   A: Yes, I have. I had to go to hospital.

4 Q: ....

   A: Yes, twice. And the weather was wonderful both times.

5 Q: ....

   A: Yes, I have. But no one could understand me.

6 Q: ....

   A: No, I haven't. It's much too expensive.

7 Q: ....

   A: Yes, I have – when I was a small child.

8 Q: ....

   A: Only once. It was really exciting.

TRANSLATION

Translate into your own language:

1 We've just had a baby. It was born
  at three o'clock this morning.

....

....

2 – What do you think of Budapest?
  – I don't know. I've never been there.

....

....

4 – Have you finished that book yet?
  – No. I've only just started it.

....

....

Now cover up the left-hand side, and translate your sentences back into English.

LISTENING: Have you ever...?

Five people answer questions about their experiences.

1 Listen and guess what the questions were.

1 Have you ever ....?

2 Have you ever ....?

3 Have you ever ....?

4 Have you ever ....?

5 Have you ever ....?

2 Listen again and complete the table.

	The speaker has/hasn't...	When was it?	Did he/she enjoy it?
1			
2			
3			
4			
5			

3 Which speaker mentions these things? What does he/she say about them?

a a square ....

b a birthday ....

c the stage ....

d money ....

e the Old Vic theatre ....

PRONUNCIATION: Falling intonation

1 In most sentences, the voice falls on the main stress. Listen to the examples.

No.

Yes.

Good.

I'm John.

It's raining.

What's your name?

They've gone to the cinema.

2 Look at these sentences. How do you think they are said? Mark the main stress with an arrow like this ＼ :

a I live in London.

b We need more petrol.

c Give it to me.

d The matches are in the cupboard.

e What are they doing?

f We've just bought a new house.

g They're watching television.

Now listen to the tape. Then practise saying the sentences.

DICTATION

You will hear part of the text from *Headline news* (Classroom Book, page 69).

Listen and write down what you hear.

READING: Varieties of English

1 What kinds of writing are these texts? Which of them is

a a note? ....

b the blurb on a book cover? ....

c a job application letter? ....

d a newspaper article? ....

e a personal letter? ....

f part of a novel? ....

2 Which texts do these questions refer to? What are the answers?

a Has he finished decorating his house? ....

b Is the fire now under control? ....

c Is their relationship finished? ....

d How many novels has she written? ....

e What job is he applying for? ....

f Who's been abroad? Did he enjoy it? ....

❶ David came to stay at the weekend. He's just come back from a trip to Algeria, where he set up some computer equipment. Algiers, I think it was, but he was a bit vague about it. Anyway, he sounds as if he had a really good time there and

❷ Although my degree was in Russian studies, I have taught both English and History, and I have a post-graduate teaching diploma. I should add that I also ran my own small business for several years, so I know a considerable amount about Business English. I would

❸ John and Helen

There wasn't any paint left for the doors, so I've gone to buy some more – I'll be back around 6. I've taken the car – sorry! There's a pizza in the fridge for the children's supper – could you heat it up for them when they come in? Thanks.

Mike

❹ Margaret Kyle was born in New York in 1955, and wrote her first novel, *Wildfire*, in 1976, while she was still at college. Since then, she has published four more novels and two collections of short stories. She now lives in Los Angeles, where she teaches modern American literature at UCLA. Margaret Kyle is married, and has three children.

❺ Fires were still raging over large areas near Kavala in Northern Greece yesterday, as the Government brought in army units to help fight the blaze. So far the fire has destroyed about 8000 hectares of forest, and attempts to control it using fire-fighting aircraft have been unsuccessful. Nearly 500 people have fled their homes in the area and have found temporary accommodation in Kavala and other nearby towns. Police have warned travellers to avoid the area, as they expect the fire to continue for several days.

❻ "Look, Alison," he said, quietly. "Things change. People change – and we've changed too. At least, I have."

"Changed? You?" She laughed harshly. He turned away, avoiding her eye, and stared out of the window.

"It's no good," he said. "I've made up my mind. I'm not coming back."

16 Free time

A Two kinds of activities

Read about Alison's and Barbara's leisure activities, and fill the gaps.

Alison's very musical. She sings and plays the (1▶), and most evenings she goes (3▶) with her friends in the local disco. She likes eating in restaurants, but she also enjoys (4▶) her own meals. She can (2▶), and has made quite a few jumpers and scarves. Alison also (5▶) stamps, and she enjoys (6▶) detective stories.

Barbara goes (7▶) every morning in the park. She enjoys athletics, especially the high-(8▶). She is also a great (9▶) fan, and goes to watch her team play every weekend. She enjoys horse-(10▶), and often plays a round of (11▶) at her local club. Barbara is a good driver, and goes (12▶)-racing whenever she can. When she's at home, you'll usually find her out in the (13▶), watering the flowers or cutting the grass.

The main difference between Alison and Barbara is that Alison enjoys (A▼) activities, whereas Barbara enjoys (B▼) activities.

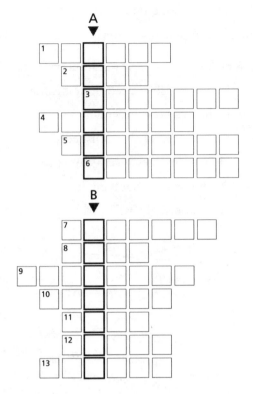

B Go, play and do

Fill the gaps below with a suitable form of *go*, *play* or *do*.

1 I don't .... tennis very well because I don't .... enough practice.

2 He doesn't .... a lot of running – he .... jogging about once a month.

3 My sister enjoys .... chess, but I don't think she's ever .... Scrabble.

4 – We're .... swimming. Do you want to come?

 – No thanks. I'm .... basketball in two hours. And I .... swimming yesterday.

5 I .... some gardening yesterday morning, and then in the afternoon we all .... sailing; and in the evening we sat at home and .... cards.

C Likes and dislikes

Talk about leisure activities that you like and don't like. Say why.

Examples:

I enjoy listening to music. It helps me to relax.
I don't like playing computer games. I think they're very boring. And I never win.

	Like/enjoy + ing or noun	
I	like don't like enjoy don't enjoy	swimming. (playing) golf. (watching) TV. eating out.

1 ....

....

2 ....

....

3 ....

....

4 ....

....

New words

Use this space to write down new words from the unit, with your own notes and examples.

....

....

....

....

....

....

....

....

....

....

....

....

....

....

TRANSLATION

Translate into your own language:

1 – Are you going to the football match?
  – No, I think I'll stay at home and
    watch it on television.

....

....

....

2 We don't do much reading these
  days. We're too busy working.

....

....

3 – How about a game of chess?
  – I'm afraid I don't know how to play.

....

....

4 I really enjoy playing the piano, but
  I'm not very good at it.

....

....

Now cover up the left-hand side, and translate your sentences back into English.

LISTENING: Rock climbing

You will hear a woman talking about rock climbing.

1 Listen to the first part. Which of these statements
  are the same as what she says? (Write ✔ or ✗).

☐ a Rock climbing is interesting because you
     have to solve problems all the time.

☐ b Rock climbing is very strenuous and it
     needs a lot of endurance.

☐ c Hill walking is more strenuous than
     rock climbing.

☐ d Climbing small rocks is surprisingly easy.

☐ e Even easy climbs can be surprisingly
     absorbing.

☐ f Rock climbing is very different from
     most other sports.

2 In the second part, the woman talks about the time she
  was most frightened. Listen and choose the picture that
  matches her description best.

3 Write two sentences that could go in the bubble.

SOUND AND SPELLING: Words with r

You have already looked at some words
with r: e.g. car, her, first, shore, turn.

Here are some new groups.

1 Listen to these words on the tape.
  Group A: /eə/   stair, chair, wear, share
  Group B: /ɪə/   cheer, clear, appear, here
  Group C: /aɪə/   wire, tired, flier, higher
  Group D: /auə/   our, flour, shower
  Group E: /juə/   pure, curious, secure

2 How do you say these words? Mark them A,
  B, C, D or E. Then listen to the tape.

☐ flower		☐ during
☐ hear		☐ we're
☐ they're		☐ fire
☐ cure		☐ where
☐ hour		☐ near
☐ hair		☐ drier

3 You will hear four sentences. Cover this
  page, and write them down.

DICTATION

You will hear part of the recording from
Leisure activities (Classroom Book, page 72).

Listen and write down what you hear.

WRITING SKILLS: Sequence (2)

1 The words in the box below are used for showing sequence.
Find them in the texts and underline them.

first
then
and
after (a few minutes)
(an hour) later

> First we drove for a few miles along the main road, and then we turned down a narrow lane. Half an hour later we came to an old farmhouse.

> We went into the football stadium and found our seats. After about ten minutes, the crowd started cheering and the two teams came onto the pitch. A few minutes later the match began.

2 Rewrite these sentences with correct punctuation.

a I first met him at a party in London ....

about a year later I saw him again ....

b She put the phone down after a few ....

seconds she picked it up again and ....

dialled a number ....

3 Fill the gaps with sequence expressions from the box.

a We bought a programme .... found our seats. .... the

curtains opened .... the play began.

b A man went into the house .... closed the door. .... he

came out again carrying a black box.

c .... I had a long, hot bath, ... I sat in bed

.... read a book. .... I fell asleep.

4 Put this story in the correct order. Use sequence expressions to join the ideas together.

Monica knew exactly what to do.
The taxi arrived.
Edward arrived home.
She packed a small suitcase.
She called a taxi.
Monica closed the door and posted her keys through the letter box.
She wrote a letter and put it on the table.
The letter said 'Goodbye, Edward. I've had enough.'

Monica knew exactly what to do.

....

....

....

....

....

....

....

....

....

....

....

....

17 Obligation

A Obligation structures

Fill the gaps with expressions from the box.

must have to	mustn't can't
don't have to	can

Must(n't), (don't) have to, can('t)	
You **must** go	
You **have to** go	= Go!
You **mustn't** go	
You **can't** go	= Don't go!

You **don't**
  have to go
	= Don't go if you
	  don't want to.

You **can** go	= Go if you want to.

1 – What time do you .... be home?

– I've got a key. I .... stay out as late as I like.

2 It's a secret. You .... tell anyone.

3 You .... take one pill three times a day. And you .... drink any alcohol.

4 Oh no! Is that the time? I .... go!

5 I love Sundays. I .... get up and I .... go to work. I .... lie in bed until lunch time if I want.

6 – .... I have a bath, please?

– Yes, of course you .... But you .... use too much hot water.

B Childish questions

Imagine you're a child in these situations. Ask questions with *Can ...?* or *Do ... have to ...?*
Example:
Your parents want to watch the news, and you want to watch *Disneytime.*
Can we watch Disneytime? or *Do we have to watch the news?*

1 You don't want to go to the dentist's.

....

2 You want chips for lunch, not a salad.

....

3 It's time for your friend to go home now.

....

4 It's bedtime for you and your brother.

....

5 It's pouring with rain, and your mother tells you it's time to go to school.

....

C Flying rules

Here are some questions about flying from someone who has never been in a plane.
What information can you give? (If you're not sure, ask someone yourself.)

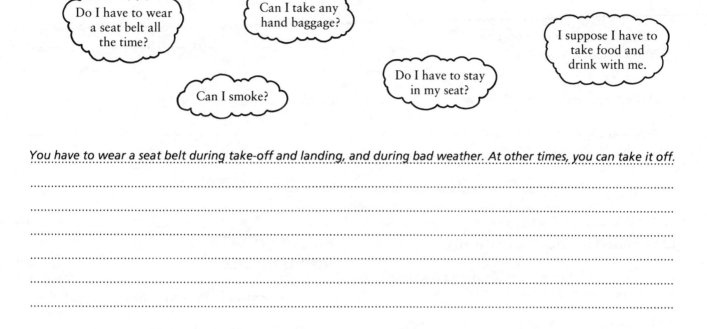

You have to wear a seat belt during take-off and landing, and during bad weather. At other times, you can take it off.

....

....

....

....

....

....

D Giving advice

Finish these sentences with some good advice. For each
one, take two ideas from the box, and add one of your own.
Use *ought (not) to* and *should(n't)*.

arrive late	drink alcohol	take exercise
be polite	eat fatty food	wear a seat belt
dress smartly	smoke	work hard

should + *infinitive*		
ought + to + *infinitive*		
You	should ought to	give it back.
You	shouldn't ought not to	keep it.

1 If you want to pass an interview, *you should dress smartly, and you shouldn't arrive late.* ....

   And you ought to ask some intelligent questions at the end. ....

2 If you want a healthy heart, ...

   ....

   ....

   ....

3 If you want to drive safely, ...

   ....

   ....

   ....

4 If you want to run a successful business, ...

   ....

   ....

   ....

TRANSLATION

Translate into your own language:

1 – My shoulder still hurts.
  – You ought to see a doctor about it.

....

....

2 – Can we have guests in our rooms?
  – Yes you can, but they have to be
    out by midnight.

....

....

....

3 DO NOT LEAN OUT OF THE WINDOW

....

4 He doesn't have to pay income
  tax – he doesn't earn enough.

....

....

Now cover up the left-hand side, and translate your sentences back into English.

LISTENING: Radio phone-in

You will hear part of a radio phone-in programme, in which two experts give advice to listeners.

1 Listen to Susan's problem. Find five differences between this text and what you hear.

Susan, who is a student, has a generally bad relationship with her husband, who has just got a new job. In the evenings he likes to go out to parties. She prefers to stay at home and read, but he won't stay with her.

a ....

b ....

c ....

d ....

e ....

2 Which of these solutions do the two experts suggest? (Write 1, 2 or – .)

a Try to talk to him.   ....

b Do what he wants.   ....

c Do what you want.   ....

d Try to compromise.   ....

e Go out with friends.   ....

f Go out with another man.   ....

g Get a divorce.   ....

3 Now mark the advice that you think is best.

PRONUNCIATION: Rising intonation

1 In some sentences, the voice *rises* at the end. This pattern is most often used in Yes/No questions. Listen to the examples and try saying them.

> Yes? ⤴
> Are you there? ⤴
> Is that you, John? ⤴
> Is it raining? ⤴
> Have you been to London? ⤴
> Did you enjoy the film? ⤴

2 Do you think these sentences have *falling* or *rising* intonation? Mark them with ⤴ or ⤵.

a Hello.

b Hello?

c Are you busy?

d My name's Peter.

e Do you drink coffee?

f Where are you going?

g He's a friend of mine.

h He's a friend of yours?

Now listen to the tape. Then practise saying the sentences.

DICTATION

You will hear most of one text from *Personal problems* (Classroom Book, page 78).

Listen and write down what you hear.

READING: Rules of the game

Which of these 'rules' for football, basketball and tennis are *true* and which are *false*?
Write T or F by each one, and then check your answers in the key.

Basketball

1 ☐ You can shoot at the basket from any part of the basketball court.

2 ☐ You mustn't run while holding the ball.

3 ☐ A game of basketball cannot result in a draw: one side must win.

4 ☐ You can stand holding the ball for as long as you like.

5 ☐ If you have committed five fouls in a single game, you must leave the game.

Football

6 ☐ For a goal to be scored, the ball must go right over the goal line, not just part of the way.

7 ☐ You mustn't deliberately touch the ball with your arm.

8 ☐ The goalkeeper mustn't leave the goal area.

9 ☐ The goalkeeper can pick up the ball anywhere on the pitch.

10 ☐ If the referee shows you a yellow card, you have to leave the pitch.

11 ☐ If the referee sees you standing in an offside position, he must blow his whistle.

12 ☐ If you deliberately push an opponent in your own goal area, the other side gets a penalty.

Tennis

13 ☐ When you serve, you have to stand behind the baseline.

14 ☐ If your first serve is out, you can have another try.

15 ☐ You have to let the ball bounce before you hit it.

16 ☐ The ball mustn't bounce more than once on your side of the net before you hit it.

17 ☐ The ball mustn't go higher than five metres.

18 ☐ If you hit your opponent with the ball, you lose the point.

19 ☐ For a ball to be 'in', it must land inside or on the line.

Key...

1 True. **2** True: you must bounce the ball while you run. **3** True: if there's a draw, you have to play extra five-minute periods until someone wins. **4** False: you must do something within five seconds. **5** True. **6** True. **7** True: you *can* touch it accidentally. **8** False: he can go anywhere on the pitch. **9** False: only in his goal area. **10** False: you must go off if he gives you a *red* card. **11** False: only if he thinks you're getting some advantage from it. **12** True (if the referee sees you). **13** True: if your foot touches the line, it's a foot fault. **14** True: you're allowed two serves. **15** False: you can hit it as soon as it's on your side of the net. **16** True. **17** False: there isn't any height limit. **18** False: it's a good way of winning the point. **19** True.

18 A day's work

A Types of work

Fill gaps 1–11 in Diagram A and Diagram B. Then read the answers to number 12.

A

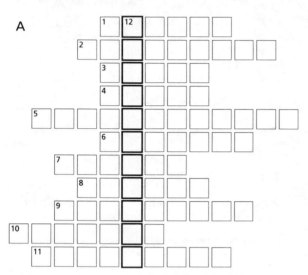

B

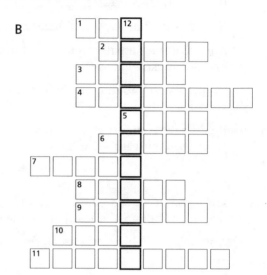

1 ▶ 'I'm a (A) officer. I arrest people who break the (B).'
2 ▶ 'I'm a (A). I type letters and I answer the (B).'
3 ▶ 'I'm an (A). I act in (B) and films.'
4 ▶ 'I'm a (A). I look after (B) in a hospital.'
5 ▶ 'I'm a hotel (A). I (B) with enquiries and reservations.'
6 ▶ 'I'm the accounts (A) for a large company. I look after the company's (B).'
7 ▶ 'I'm a hotel (A). I (B) guests' luggage for them.'
8 ▶ 'I'm a (A). I write children's (B).'
9 ▶ 'I'm a (A). I paint the inside and outside of people's (B).'
10 ▶ 'I'm a (A). I have to (B) a lot of books, and write a lot of essays.'
11 ▶ 'I'm a shop (A). I serve the (B) who come into the shop.'

12 ▼ The speakers all have different (A). They answer the question (B)?'

B Careers

Fill the gaps with a verb from the box, in the right form.
Some are used more than once.

apply	look
be	lose
enjoy	retire
get	start
leave	work

1 Last week I .... for a job in a car factory, but I didn't

.... it.

2 – Where do you .... ?

– in a shop. I only .... the job last week.

– Are you .... it?

– No, not much. I'm going to .... at the end of the week.

3 If you're not careful, you'll .... the sack.

4 He .... his job when the factory closed, so he's .... for another one.

5 I'm .... as a taxi driver at the moment.

6 She .... off as a secretary, but she .... soon promoted to sales manager.

And when the director .... in two years' time, she'll probably .... his job.

New words

Use this space to write down new words from the unit, with your own notes and examples.

....

....

....

....

....

....

....

....

....

....

....

....

....

TRANSLATION

Translate into your own language:

1 Have they got any vacancies?
   I'm looking for a job.

   ....

   ....

2 – Does she still work for Shell?
   – No, she retired last year.

   ....

   ....

3 I don't earn very much, but I
   enjoy the work and I get long
   holidays.

   ....

   ....

   ....

4 I'm writing to apply for the job
   you advertised in the *Times*.

   ....

   ....

Now cover up the left-hand side, and translate your sentences back into English.

LISTENING: A security guard

You will hear an interview with a security guard who works
for a company called *Securicor*.

1 Listen to the first part and complete these
   sentences.

   Securicor guards are hired by ....

   ....

   Their job is to guard ....

   ....

   They prevent ....

   ....

2 Before you listen to the second part, try to guess
   how the man would answer these questions.

   Write *Yes* or *No*.

   a Is the work varied?   ....

   b Do you meet people in your job?   ....

   c Is it interesting?   ....

   d Is it well paid?   ....

   e Can you earn overtime pay?   ....

   f Do you have to work at night? ....

   g Do you get much free time?   ....

3 Listen and check your answers.

SOUND AND SPELLING: Hard and soft *c* and *g*

1 Listen to these words on the tape.
   Hard c: /k/   camera, cost, cut, back, fact
   Soft c: /s/   cent, city, receive, icy, dancing
   Hard g: /g/   garden, gun, pig, foggy, again,
                  ugly
   Soft g: /dʒ/ page, large, judge, changing,
                  pigeon

2 How do you say these words? Mark them
   H (hard) or S (soft). Then listen.

☐	ceiling	☐	figure
☐	orange	☐	secret
☐	copy	☐	agent
☐	capital	☐	piece
☐	fence	☐	apricot
☐	magazine	☐	fridge

3 You will hear four sentences. Cover this
   page, and write them down.

DICTATION

You will hear two of the texts from
Occupations (Classroom Book, page 80).
Listen and write down what you hear.

WRITING SKILLS: Letter writing

1 How we end a letter depends on how we begin it. Look at the examples in the box.

2 Match the beginnings and endings of the letters below.
   Who's writing to:

   a Boyd's?   ....

   b Susan?   ....

   c Cosmos?   ....

   d Tom?   ....

Beginning	Ending
Dear Sir Dear Madam Dear Sir/Madam	Yours faithfully
Dear Ms Jones Dear Mr King Dear Mrs Marple	Yours sincerely
Dear Tom Dear Fiona	Best wishes Yours Love

Yours faithfully,
Elizabeth Burke

Yours sincerely,
Douglas Trafford

Yours,
Miranda

The Manager,
Boyd's Bookshop,
15 College Rd.,
Bristol BR4 6LU

Dear Sir/Madam,

I am writing to complain about who was extremely rude to me on

Lots of love,
Don
x x x

Ms P. Williams,
Cosmos Travel,
5 New St.,
Cardiff CF3 2BD

Dear Ms Williams,

Thank you for sending arrived yesterday. I have

Dear Susan,

I just had to write to can't stop thinking abo. such a wonderful time I want so much to stay

Dear Tom,
So sorry not to have written for so long. but I've had rather a hectic few weeks at

3 You have seen this advertisement in the newspaper. Write a letter asking for more details, and saying briefly who you are and why you are interested. Use the letter format given.

WORK ABROAD and learn a language at the same time. No experience necessary.
Write for details to:
Interchange, P.O.Box 532, Amsterdam, The Netherlands.

```
                          Your address
                                Date
Address you're
writing to

Dear...



            (Your letter)






Ending
```

Revision and extension

1 Sentences

Complete the sentences.
Example:
It's getting late. *I must go* home soon.

1 You can stay out late if you like. You

.... come home early.

2 Spanish isn't very difficult – in fact, it's the

.... I've ever learnt.

3 Duck is .... chicken,

but it's cheaper than steak.

4 I'm still looking for my wallet – I

.... yet.

5 – I'm terribly overweight.

– Well, you .... so

much.

6 – Do you like English mustard?

– I don't know. I ....

tried it.

7 You can smoke in the cafeteria, but

.... smoke in the

classrooms.

2 Asking questions

Complete the questions.
Example:
– *Have you finished* your lunch?
– No, I'm still eating it.

1 – .... John or

Richard?

– Richard's taller, I think.

2 – .... wear a suit?

– No you don't. You can wear whatever you like.

3 – .... the way to

the nearest bank?

– Yes. There's one just round the corner.

4 – .... skiing?

– Yes, I love it, but I'm not very good at it.

5 – .... tennis?

– No I haven't, but I've played table-tennis.

6 – .... yet?

– No, they're still asleep.

7 – .... still

.... for *Argos Travel*?

– Yes I am – I'm the assistant manager now.

3 Prepositions

Fill the gaps with prepositions from the box.

1 Have you ever been .... a jazz concert?

2 She resigned .... her old job and now she's

applying .... a new one.

3 I'm looking .... my keys. Have you seen

them anywhere?

4 She studied chemistry .... university.

5 Turn right .... the traffic lights and you'll

see the house .... the end .... the

road.

after	from	out of
at	into	to
for	of	with

6 Please do not throw bottles .... the window.

7 Johnson kicked the ball straight past the goalkeeper

.... the net.

8 I work .... a package tour company. I look

.... the tourists and deal .... any

problems they have.

4 Word order

Put these jumbled sentences in the right order. Remember to begin each
sentence with a capital letter.

Example:
worked hotel ever he a has in ?
Has he ever worked in a hotel?

1 more to they any theatre go don't the .

....

2 you to to time work have what get do ?

....

3 guide working enjoy she as tourist a doesn't .

....

4 and road go right this down turn straight .

....

5 nurses money doctors than more earn .

....

6 think Europe the city in I is beautiful Prague most .

....

5 Writing paragraphs

Write a short paragraph (2 or 3 sentences) on the following:

1 Imagine you've just won some money. Write part of a letter telling a friend the news.

....

....

....

2 What do you do in your free time? Write about one indoor activity and one outdoor activity.

....

....

....

3 Imagine you're a hotel receptionist. Say what you do in your job.

....

....

....

4 What is there to do in your town in the evenings?

....

....

....

19 Narration

A What were they doing?

There was an electricity cut yesterday evening. What do you think these people were doing when it happened? Complete the sentences using the Past continuous.

Spelling of -ing forms

watch (+ ing) → watching
change (¢ + ing) → changing
have (¢ + ing) → having
run (+ n + ing) → running

1 Helen *was writing a letter on her word processor.*

(The screen suddenly went blank.)

2 The Smiths ....

(They missed the end of their programme.)

3 John ....

(He couldn't find his towel in the dark.)

4 Pamela ....

(She finished it by candlelight.)

5 The Browns ....

(Luckily they had a gas cooker.)

6 Lucia ....

(She put on her jumper back to front.)

7 George ....

(He cut himself.)

8 Terry ....

(He had to finish it later.)

9 Karen ....

(What a pity! She was winning, too!)

B Short stories

Tell stories based on the information in the table. For each story, choose one item from A and one item from B. Say when it happened, and what happened next.

Example:

I was driving to work yesterday morning when I felt a sudden pain in my leg. I stopped the car quickly and got out, and saw a bee on the driver's seat.

A	B
wait for a train	smell smoke
get into the bath	hear someone say 'Hello!'
cook breakfast	hear a shot
walk in a forest	lose [my/her/his ...] balance
drive to work	see the headline in the paper
practise the piano	look at [my/her/his ...] watch
paint the ceiling	feel a sudden pain

1 ....

....

....

....

2 ....

....

....

3 ....

....

....

....

C ...-ing ...-ing ...

What do you remember about the street scene in Unit 18 of the Classroom Book? Use *two* expressions from the box (changing them to *-ing* forms) to complete each sentence.

carry two suitcases	sing
carry some bricks	sit by the road
come out of a hotel	sit in a café
dig a hole in the road	stand by a piano
drink coffee	stand by a car
look at the engine	stand on the pavement
play a saxophone	wear a helmet

1 There was a workman   *standing on the pavement, carrying some bricks.* ....

2 There was a porter ....

3 A young woman was ....

4 In the street there was a man ....

5 Upstairs there was a woman ....

6 A mechanic was ....

7 Two men were ....

TRANSLATION

Translate into your own language:

1 – How did you break your leg?
   – I fell off a ladder.

....

....

2 We first met in Paris. I was
   visiting my uncle at the time.

....

....

3 I was sitting at a table having a cup of
   coffee when someone shouted 'Fire!'

....

....

4 He wasn't feeling well, so he left.

....

Now cover up the left-hand side, and translate your sentences back into English.

LISTENING: Two stories

You will hear two stories. Story A is about a wedding. Story B is about football hooligans.

1 Before you listen, guess which words you think appear in each story. Mark them A or B.

☐	carriage	☐	reception
☐	embarrassing	☐	supporters
☐	frightened	☐	terrifying
☐	groom	☐	underground
☐	noise	☐	video
☐	platform	☐	wallet

Now listen to the tape, and check your answers.

2 Listen again and complete the stories.

Story A: The speaker went to a friend's .... They made a .... of their ...., and later they .... him round to watch it. While watching it, he noticed the .... of the .... stealing someone's .... It was very ....

Story B: The speaker was sitting in .... when a crowd of .... got in. First they made a lot of .... Then they started rocking the .... She felt very ...., and got out as soon as the .... opened. Then she burst into ....

PRONUNCIATION: Intonation: questions

1 We usually use *rising intonation*:
   – in Yes/No questions
   – if we want something repeated
   We usually use *falling intonation*:
   – in Wh- questions
   Listen to the examples.

> 1 Is Mary at home? ↗
>   Yes, she is. ↘
> 2 What's the time? ↘
>   About six o'clock. ↘
> 3 I come from Portsmouth. ↘
>   Where? ↗

2 Mark these sentences with ↘ or ↗.

   a – Can you ski?
        – Yes, I can.
   b – My car's broken down.
        – Oh, has it really?
   c – My name's Mifanwy.
        – Pardon?
   d – Did you see the film last night?
        – Yes, I did.
        – What did you think of it?

Now listen to the tape. Then practise saying the sentences.

DICTATION

You will hear part of the text from *Setting a scene* (Classroom Book, page 88).

Listen and write down what you hear.

READING: Bad luck

Here are two stories about bad luck. Put the sentences in the right order.

Superstition

1 ...*H*...　2 ....　3 ....　4 ....　5 ....

6 ....　7 ....　8 ....　9 ....

A 'I'll never be superstitious again,' she said.

B Then she stepped off the pavement to avoid walking under a ladder and a bicycle knocked her over.

C She believed that Friday was an unlucky day, and that thirteen was an unlucky number.

D It was Friday the thirteenth.

E One day she stopped to stroke a black cat on a wall and it scratched her face.

F Then she looked at the calendar.

G She arrived home with her face bleeding and her leg bruised.

H Sue was very superstitious.

I She thought that black cats brought good luck, and never walked under a ladder if she could help it.

The Thief

1 ...*C*...　2 ....　3 ....　4 ....

5 ....　6 ....　7 ....　8 ....

A Now they could do whatever they liked: no one could prove anything.

B They knew!

C The train came in, and Jake followed two elderly women into the nearest compartment.

D Jake quietly took the bag out of his pocket and dropped it out of the window.

E It was then that he saw the *No Smoking* sign in the window.

F As they left the station, he noticed one of the women staring at him over her newspaper.

G He had a bag of stolen jewels in his pocket, and he lit up a cigarette to steady his nerves.

H Then, to his horror, he heard them whispering something about calling the guard.

Adapted from **Micro Stories** *by Josephine Jones (Wida Software)*

20 | People

A Physical appearance

Use the words in the boxes to describe the people in the story.

I got on the train, and found my seat. There was only one other person in the compartment. He _was a short man in his 30s with curly black hair and a moustache. He was wearing a brown raincoat_. Just before the train left the station, a woman came into our compartment and sat down opposite me. She ....

....

....

At the next station, an elderly man got in and sat in the corner. He

....

....

....

....

The next station was mine. I got off the train and telephoned Mrs Chadwick. 'I'll come and meet you in five minutes,' she said. 'How will I recognise you?' 'Well,' I said, 'I'm ....

....

....

....

.... ,

black	moustache
short	30s
curly hair	brown
raincoat	

green	tall	short
fair	sunglasses	
hair	dress	20s

beard	blue	grey
walking stick	70s	
short	bald	eyes

Describe yourself.

B Character adjectives

Match the sentences with the words in the box.

☐	shy	☐	generous
☐	selfish	1	friendly
☐	modest	☐	self-confident
☐	mean	☐	bad-tempered
☐	honest	☐	easy-going
☐	lazy	☐	hard-working

1 ... always smiles and says hello when we meet.
2 ... doesn't like giving away money.
3 ... gets angry quite a lot.
4 ... is afraid to speak to strangers.
5 ... isn't afraid to speak to strangers.
6 ... usually stays late at the office.
7 ... always tells the truth.
8 ... doesn't get upset if things go wrong.
9 ... doesn't work very hard.
10 ... always brings you a little present.
11 ... doesn't boast.
12 ... is only interested in himself/herself.

New words

Use this space to write down new words from the unit, with your own notes and examples.

....
....
....
....
....
....
....
....
....
....
....
....
....

TRANSLATION

Translate into your own language:

1 – She's still in her 20s.
  – Is she? She looks older than that.

....

....

2 He was a tall, thin man with long, fair hair and a moustache, and he always wore a leather jacket.

....

....

....

3 – Do you always wear glasses?
  – No, only for driving.

....

....

4 He's one of the most generous people I've ever met.

....

....

Now cover up the left-hand side, and translate your sentences back into English.

LISTENING: Famous people

You will hear three people describing (1) Queen Victoria, (2) Napoleon and (3) Indira Gandhi.

1 Here are some of the things they say.
Before you listen: Which phrases do you think go with each person? Write V, N or G.

a ☐ very impressive looking

b ☐ always wore black

c ☐ always wore a uniform

d ☐ didn't often laugh

e ☐ wore a three-pointed hat

f ☐ lived to a very old age

g ☐ had a very striking face

h ☐ a very peaceful looking person

i ☐ hair tied in a tight bun

j ☐ was dark-skinned and had greying hair

k ☐ had dark hair and dark eyes

l ☐ had a small mouth and quite a pointed chin

2 Listen to the tape and check your answers.

SOUND AND SPELLING: Long and short vowels

1 Listen to these words on the tape.

Words with short vowels

bad	get	sit	stop	fun
rabbit	getting	dinner	stopped	sunny

Words with long vowels

late	hide	hope	amuse
latest	hiding	hotel	used

2 Here are some words that you probably don't know. How do you think they are said? Mark them S (short) or L (long). Then listen to the tape.

☐	mute	☐	glutton
☐	coping	☐	scraper
☐	scram	☐	flitted
☐	pane	☐	inducing
☐	strive	☐	spottiest
☐	petty	☐	refinery

3 You will hear four sentences. Write them down.

DICTATION

You will hear three parts of the reading text from *The Dream Game* (Classroom Book, page 93).

Listen and write down what you hear.

WRITING SKILLS: Relative clauses (1)

1 Here are two parts of a letter written by a foreign student in Paris.

I'm staying with my uncle. He lives just outside Paris. He's got a large house, with a beautiful garden.	My uncle is quite rich. He works for Inter Export. It's a large company based in Paris.

We can join the sentences in each paragraph like this:

I'm staying with my uncle, **who** lives just outside Paris. He's got a large house, with a beautiful garden.	My uncle is quite rich. He works for Inter Export, **which** is a large company based in Paris.

We use *who* to talk about people.
We use *which* to talk about things.
Before *who* or *which* we write a comma (,).

2 These sentences all have mistakes. Rewrite them correctly.

a I live in Stenton, it's a small village near Cambridge.

....

....

b I've got three sisters, which are all older than me.

....

....

c I've got a younger brother. Who's in the army.

....

....

d Pandas, which they only eat bamboo, are becoming very rare.

....

....

> She's studying art here.
> It's a kind of sausage.
> It still isn't very good.
> They're also staying in Paris.
> It was built in the 70s.
> It's about 200 km south of here.

3 Here are some more sentences from the student's letter. Fill the gaps with information from the box. Use *who* or *which*.

a I'm sending you a picture of the Pompidou Centre, ...

What do you think of it?

b Last night I met some old schoolfriends, ... We went out

for a meal together.

c I had a very interesting dish called *andouillette*, ...

d George sends you his best wishes. He's staying in Lyon, ...

e I'm spending a lot of time with a girl called Mona, ...

I met her at a party last weekend.

f I'm doing everything I can to improve my French, ...

21 Prediction

A Will, might & won't

Choose topics from the box, and make three predictions for the next ten years:
one with *will (probably)*, one with *might* and one with *(probably) won't*.

Example: *my life*

I'll probably get married. I might go and live abroad. I probably
won't have any children.

my life
politics
sport
my family
television
science

1 Topic: ....

....

....

2 Topic: ....

....

....

3 Topic: ....

....

....

B Questions with 'will'

Ask questions with *will*. Some are Yes/No questions, and some are Wh- questions.

Examples:

Mexico City might win tonight, or they might not. → *Will Mexico City win tonight?*

There might be 20 people at the party. Or 30. Or ... → *How many people will there be at the party?*

1 The train might arrive at 2.00, or at 2.30, or ...

....

2 It might be windy tomorrow, or it might not.

....

3 There might be a general election this year, or there might not.

....

4 You might be at home, or at work, or ...

....

5 I might see you again tomorrow, or next week, or ...

....

6 They might lend us the money, or they might not.

....

7 The ticket might cost me £10, or £20, or ...

....

C If & unless

Write sentences with *if* or *unless* based on these pieces of advice.

> **unless = if ... not ...**
>
> **If you post it now, it'll probably get there on time.**
> **If you *don't* post it now, it won't get there on time.**
> ***Unless* you post it now, it won't get there on time.**

Examples:

You ought to complain about it. → *If you complain, they'll give you a new one.*
You should book a seat for the concert. → *You won't get in unless you book a seat.*

1 You should wear a raincoat when you go out.

....

2 You ought to leave before dark.

....

3 You ought to apologise.

....

4 You should phone your parents.

....

5 You should go to bed early tonight.

....

6 Don't forget his birthday.

....

7 You ought to have a holiday.

....

D Predictions with 'going to'

Complete each item with a prediction with *going to*.
Example: There isn't a cloud in the sky. ...

> *It's going to be a beautiful day.*
> *It's not going to rain.*
> *It's going to be a cold night.*
> *There are going to be lots of stars tonight.*

1 Look at all those dark clouds in the sky. ...

....

2 She's pregnant. She's ...

....

3 Oh dear. Have you got a tissue? I think ...

....

4 I've eaten too many chocolates. I think ...

....

5 That plane's flying much too low. ...

....

6 You haven't done enough work for your exam. ...

....

7 And he's a long way in front of the others now! ...

....

8 He's had a car accident. But don't worry – ...

....

TRANSLATION

Translate into your own language:

1 They'll probably just ask you a few questions. And they might take your photograph.

....

....

....

2 – How long will it take to get there?
  – About a quarter of an hour if we walk quickly.

....

....

....

3 I haven't got any money on me – I'll have to write you a cheque.

....

....

Now cover up the left-hand side, and translate your sentences back into English.

LISTENING: Driving test

You will hear a woman explaining what to expect when taking a driving test in Britain.

1 Here are some things the instructor will say during the test. In what order does the woman mention them? Listen and number the remarks from 1 to 7.

Stop!

Well, I'm glad to say you've passed your test.

OK, off you go.

What did that road sign say?

Turn right at the crossroads.

Park the car just here.

Which is your car?

2 Listen again and answer these questions.

  a Where do you take the driving test?
  b What is the first thing you do when you get in the car?
  c What does the instructor have with him?
  d What does the pink paper mean?

PRONUNCIATION: Contrastive stress

1 We can change the meaning of a sentence by changing the stress. Listen to the examples.

> I like playing <u>foot</u>ball.
> I like playing <u>foot</u>ball.
> *(but not tennis)*
> I like <u>play</u>ing football.
> *(but not watching it)*
> <u>I</u> like playing football.
> *(but my brother doesn't)*

2 How do you say these sentences? Underline the main stress

  a She was a maths teacher.
    (not a history teacher)

  b She was a maths teacher.
    (she works in a library now)

  c My mother usually gets up early.
    (but the rest of us stay in bed)

  d My mother usually gets up early.
    (but not always)

  e I didn't see him yesterday.
    (it was three days ago)

  f I didn't see him yesterday.
    (I spoke to him on the phone)

  Now listen to the tape.

DICTATION

You will hear two parts of the text from *What will it be like?* (Classroom Book, page 94).

Listen and write down what you hear.

READING: Star gazing

1 What can people born under these four star signs expect this week?
Write the first letter of each star sign L (= Libra), S, P and/or T.

Who might expect ...

a a romantic evening? ....

b to hear about other
people's problems? ....

c to hear from a long
lost friend? ....

d an interesting week
at work ....

e to win an argument? ....

f money troubles? ....

g to get some money? ....

h a plan to go wrong? ....

i something nice to
happen on Tuesday? ....

j a problem with
someone in the
family? ....

2 Which horoscope would you

a most like to be yours? ....

b least like to be yours? ....

YOUR FUTURE IN THE STARS | Paul Zak reveals what the week has in store

LIBRA
23 September–21 October

If you've been on holiday this week, you might find that you don't want to go back to work – who does? But an unexpected visit will cheer you up, and there may be a letter or a long-distance phone call from a relative or friend. Someone close to you suddenly changes their mind, and you find you've won a long-standing argument without saying a word. At home, something you've planned doesn't work out, but don't worry – everything will turn out all right in the end.

☆ Be careful what you say on Friday.

PISCES
20 February–20 March

You'll be occupied with worries about your home and family this week. You may be having problems paying the bills, or perhaps someone isn't doing all they can to help around the house. It's a problem that can be solved – but it's up to you to do it. This would also be a good time to sit down and write all those letters you've been putting off. Friends might bring their problems to you too: you can help, but you should sort out your own problems first.

☆ A lucky break on Tuesday.

SAGITTARIUS
23 November–21 December

Lots of things go right this week. A friend you haven't seen for years turns up out of the blue, and you sort out an old family quarrel. Your love-life goes well too – you can look forward to a great night out, and something you've been dreaming of for years actually comes true. At work, someone tries to make things difficult for you, but who cares? There are good times ahead, so forget about work and enjoy yourself.

☆ Don't make any big decisions on Monday.

TAURUS
21 April–21 May

If you're planning to spend your money having fun this week, better forget it – you've got some big bills coming. But there's no need to worry: if you're careful, you should be able to sort things out fairly quickly – and you might even end up richer than when you started. At work, you have an opportunity to show what you can do: make the most of it.

☆ An enjoyable meeting on Tuesday.

---

22 Around the world

A On the map

Write the missing words in the diagram. Then complete sentence number 12.

1 .... Victoria is in East Africa; .... Superior is in Canada. (4)
2 Asia is one; Europe is another; Africa is another. (9)
3 Vesuvius is a ....; so is Etna; and Popocatepetl; and Krakatoa. (7)
4 The Danube is a ....; so is the Thames; and the Amazon. (5)
5 The Niagara falls are on the U.S.–Canada ....(6)
6 An area full of trees, such as the Black .... in Germany. (6)
7 The Atlantic, for example; or the Pacific; or the Indian. (5)
8 Fuji, for example; or the Matterhorn; or Kilimanjaro. (8)
9 A dry region, such as the Sahara, the Gobi, and the Kalahari. (6)
10 Sri Lanka is an ....; so is Cyprus; and Tahiti. (6)
11 San Francisco is on the West .... of the U.S.A. (5)

12▼ Answers 1–11 are all part of the ....

B A good place to visit

A friend has asked you to recommend a good place to go for a holiday in your country. Write part of a letter, in which you answer these questions:

What's the place called? Where is it?

What's the surrounding area like?

What can you do there?

What's the weather like?

What's the best time of year to go there?

....
....
....
....
....
....
....
....

C International quiz

The answers to all the questions are countries, nationalities or languages.

1 Which countries are these the capital cities of?

a Edinburgh ....

b Bangkok ....

c Ankara ....

d Budapest ....

e Dublin ....

f Vienna ....

2 What nationality are the speakers?

a 'I'm from Rio de Janiero.' ....

b 'I'm from Lisbon.' ....

c 'I'm from Toronto.' ....

d 'I'm from Johannesburg.' ....

e 'I'm from Warsaw.' ....

f 'I'm from Copenhagen.' ....

3 What languages do these words come from?

a karate ....

b pizza ....

c champagne ....

d sauna ....

e perestroika ....

4 Here is *Do you speak ...?* in six different languages. What languages are they?

a ¿Hablas español? ....

b Spreek jij Nederlands? ....

c Sprechen Sie deutsch? ....

d هل تتكلم العربية؟ ....

e Μιλάτε ελληνικά; ....

f 你会说中文吗? ....

New words

Use this space to write down new words from the unit, with your own notes and examples.

....

....

....

....

....

....

....

....

....

....

....

....

....

TRANSLATION

Translate into your own language:

1 Her first language is Turkish, but she also speaks Arabic and Chinese.

....

....

2 No wonder I feel hot. The temperature's nearly 40° in here.

....

....

3 It's a large industrial town not far from the coast.

....

....

4 It's often quite windy here in the winter, but it hardly ever rains.

....

....

Now cover up the left-hand side, and translate your sentences back into English.

LISTENING: Living in a hot climate

You will hear a woman talking about the climate in the Arabian Gulf. Look at these questions. Then listen and note down the woman's answers. Are there any questions she *doesn't* answer?

1 Is it always hot in the Arabian Gulf?

....

2 Which are the hottest months?

....

3 When is the coolest time of year?

....

4 Is it humid?

....

5 Does it ever rain?

....

6 Are most buildings air-conditioned?

....

7 Is it too hot to drive a car?

....

8 Do you ever need warm clothes?

....

9 Is the sea pleasant to swim in?

....

SOUND AND SPELLING: Words with *s*

1 Listen to these words on the tape.
   /s/: sit, smoke, science, square
   /s/: lesson, passing, possible, escape, disturb, whisper
   /s/: class, less, makes, lights, maps, laughs
   /z/: easy, losing, wiser, thousand
   /z/: apples, goes, mends, legs, matches

2 How do you say these words? Mark them s or z. Then listen to the tape.

☐	press	☐	buys
☐	busy	☐	scream
☐	coughs	☐	climbs
☐	messy	☐	listen
☐	princes	☐	please
☐	princess	☐	trousers

3 You will hear eight words. How do you spell them? Write them down.

DICTATION

You will hear part of the text from *Visiting time* (Classroom Book, page 99).

Listen and write down what you hear.

WRITING SKILLS: Relative clauses (2)

1 Look at this information about India.

Bombay is one of India's main sea ports. (**It's** on the west coast.)

Jawaharlal Nehru died in 1964. (**He** was the first prime minister of India.)

200 kilometres from the capital Delhi is the town of Agra. (The Taj Mahal was built **there** in 1653.)

The best time to visit Agra is November-February. (The weather's not too hot **then**.)

We can join these ideas together using relative clauses:

Bombay, **which** is on the west coast, is one of India's main sea ports.

Jawaharlal Nehru, **who** was the first prime minister of India, died in 1964.

200 kilometres from the capital Delhi is the town of Agra, **where** the Taj Mahal was built in 1653.

The best time to visit Agra is November-February, **when** the weather's not too hot.

2 Join the ideas in brackets ( ) to the main sentence using a relative clause.

a Jakarta has a population of about seven million. (It's the capital of Indonesia.)

....
....
....

b The Cape Verde Islands have been independent since 1975. (They used to be a Portuguese colony.)

....
....
....

c In the Square there is a statue of Charles I. (He was King of England from 1625 to 1649.)

....
....
....

d In Alaska it can be dangerous to go out in winter. (The temperature often falls below −30°.)

....
....
....

3 Join these ideas together so that they make a paragraph of four or five sentences. Use *who*, *which*, *where* and *and*.

If you have time, you should visit the Parrot Café. It's in a small side street behind the harbour. It's the oldest café in the town. It's very popular with fishermen. They sit there all day playing cards. The owner is in his 80s. He's a retired sea captain. Next to the Parrot Café there's a small museum. You can see treasure from an old sailing ship there. It sank near the town in the 17th century.

....
....
....
....
....
....
....
....
....
....
....
....

23 Duration

A For or since?

Fill the gaps with *for* or *since*.

1 I stayed there .... two weeks when I was a student. And .... then we've gone there for our summer holiday every year.

2 We've known each other .... most of our lives, but we've only been married .... a few months.

3 Nigeria was a British colony .... more than 50 years. It has been independent .... 1960.

4 I only slept .... four hours last night – I've been up .... five o'clock this morning. I'm so tired, I think I could sleep .... a week.

5 She's been driving .... her 17th birthday, and she's now 31, so she's been driving .... 14 years.

6 He hasn't changed much. He's been living in the same house .... the 50s; he's been doing the same job .... nearly 40 years; and he's been driving the same car .... I was a boy. And he's had that moustache .... his early 20s.

B Talking about duration

Rewrite these sentences using *for* or *since*.
Examples:

He turned on the TV half an hour ago. → *He's been watching the TV for half an hour.*
I got this cold on Friday. → *I've had this cold since Friday.*

I've	had that dog	for	six months. five years. a long time.
He's	lived here		
We've	been living here	since	January. 1965. last summer.
They've	been learning French		

1 I met him at my birthday party.

....

2 She went to sleep a long time ago.

....

3 They started learning Arabic last autumn.

....

4 We got divorced six months ago.

....

5 I started reading this book yesterday lunchtime.

....

6 She got her guitar for Christmas.

....

7 He started wearing glasses five years ago.

....

C How long…?

Continue these remarks with questions with *How long …?*

Examples:

I see you've got a dog now. → *How long have you had it?*
Oh, so they've moved to London, have they? → *How long have they been living there?*

1 Oh, so you know Kate, do you?

....

2 I see he's got a cold.

....

3 I didn't know they were staying in this hotel.

....

4 Oh, so he plays the piano, does he?

....

5 Her Spanish is very good.

....

6 That's a lovely coat you're wearing.

....

7 I didn't know she was in Italy.

....

D Autobiography

Write a few sentences about your past life. Say
what you did, and say when and for how long.

Example:

*I was born in 1965. I spent the first five years of my life in
Oxford. Then we lived in London for 12 years. I went to
secondary school from 1976 till 1982. Then I studied law
at college for five years. I left college in 1987, and spent
a year travelling. Since then, I've been working as a solicitor.*

> **I spent** three years (**working**) in a bank.
> I worked in a bank **for** three years.
> I worked in a bank **from 1986 to/till 1989.**

....

....

....

....

....

....

....

....

....

TRANSLATION

Translate into your own language:

1 – You look exhausted.
  – Yes, I've been up since 6 o'clock.

....

....

2 – How long have you known each other?
  – Ages. We were at school together.

....

....

3 She's very fit. She spends at least
  two hours a day doing exercises.

....

....

4 I was there from 9 o'clock till
  lunchtime.

....

....

Now cover up the left hand side, and translate your sentences back into English.

LISTENING: 24 hours

You will hear someone saying how she spent a typical day.

1 Listen and complete the table.

Activity	How long?
a work	
b travel	
c meals	
d talking	
e reading	
f TV	
g sleep	

2 Now listen again and answer these questions.

a What is Mary's occupation?

....

b How many children has she got?

....

c Does she live a long way from the shops?

....

d What is the main meal of her day?

....

e What kind of books does she read most?

....

f How does she feel at the end of the day?

....

PRONUNCIATION: Dialogues

Look at these dialogues.

1 Underline the main stress in each sentence.
2 Mark each sentence with an arrow to show rising ⤴ or falling ⤵ intonation.
3 Which sounds are reduced to /ə/ ?

Dialogue A

– I'm going to Spain next week.
– Are you? Who are you going with?
– Mary.
– Who?

Dialogue B

– Would you like to come to the cinema tonight?
– No, I'm afraid I can't. I'm busy tonight.
– Are you free tomorrow, then?
– No, I'm busy tomorrow, too.

Dialogue C

– Have you ever been to Malaysia?
– No I haven't, but I've been to Thailand.
– Oh. Were you there on holiday?
– No, not on holiday. It was a business trip.

Now listen and check your answers.

DICTATION

You will hear three parts of the text from *A Slice of life* (Classroom Book, page 103).
Listen and write down what you hear.

READING: General knowledge quiz

How good is your general knowledge? Try these questions (choose a, b, c or d).
Then check your answers in the key.

1 In 1927, Charles Lindbergh completed the first solo flight across the Atlantic. He was in the air for about
  a 9 hours   b 17 hours
  c 25 hours   d 33 hours

2 Tokyo has been the capital city of Japan since
  a 1718   b 1768   c 1868   d 1918

3 Horses usually live for between 20 and 35 years, but they can live for as long as
  a 40–45 years   b 50–55 years
  c 60–65 years   d 70–75 years

4 The wheel is one of civilisation's oldest and most useful inventions. But how long have people been using wheeled vehicles?
  a less than 3000 years   b 3,000–4,000 years
  c 4,000–5,000 years   d more than 5000 years

5 In 1961, the Soviet astronaut Yuri Gagarin became the first man in Space. His flight lasted for
  a less than 2 hours   b 12 hours
  c 3 days   d more than 5 days

6 In Switzerland, women have had the vote since
  a 1881   b 1911   c 1941   d 1971

7 When the Sun's light reaches the Earth, it has been travelling for
  a 8½ seconds   b 85 seconds
  c 8½ minutes   d 85 minutes

8 Singapore is one of the world's smallest countries (620 square km). It's been an independent state since
  a 1945   b 1955   c 1965   d 1975

9 Agatha Christie's play *The Mousetrap* is London's longest running play. It's been running continuously since
  a 1952   b 1962   c 1972   d 1982

10 At the North Pole, it's daylight for six months of the year. But which six months?
  a   from mid-December to mid-June
  b   from mid-March to mid-September
  c   from mid-June to mid-December
  d   from mid-September to mid-March

Key
1 d The flight, from Long Island, New York, to Paris, France, was 5810 km long. Lindbergh won a $25,000 prize.

2 c Before that Kyoto was the capital.

3 c The record is held by 'Old Billy', a working horse from Lancashire, England, who lived for 62 years (1760-1822).

4 d The wheel was invented by the Sumerians in about 3300 BC. These were solid wheels: wheels with spokes appeared 1,400 years later.

5 a Gagarin's rocket left the Soviet Union on 12 April 1961, went once round the Earth , and landed again 108 minutes later. It travelled at a height of 320 km and a speed of 28,000 kph.

6 d Male voters decided to allow women to vote in a referendum held in February 1971.

7 c Light travels at 18 million km per minute, and the Sun is 150 million km from the Earth.

8 c Formerly a British Colony, Singapore was part of Malaysia from 1963 until 1965.

9 a It's a major tourist attraction. The identity of the murderer is a well kept secret.

10 b And then it's dark from mid-September to mid-March.

24 But is it art?

A People and places

Which people and places do you associate with the following? Fill the spaces with words from the box. You'll need to use some words more than once.

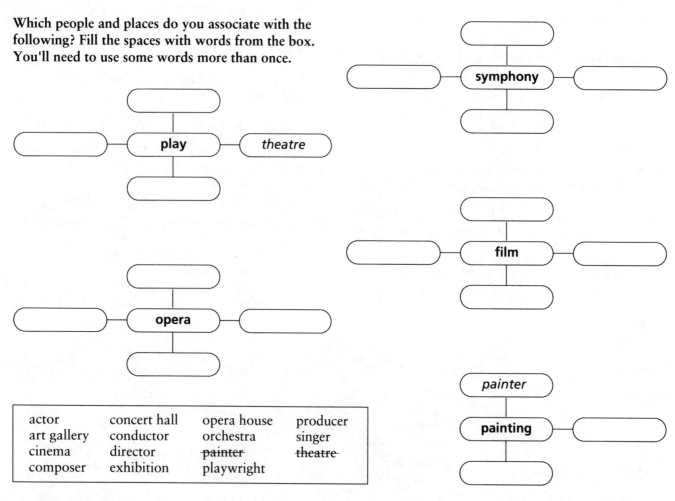

play — theatre

opera

symphony

film

painter
painting

actor	concert hall	opera house	producer
art gallery	conductor	orchestra	singer
cinema	director	~~painter~~	~~theatre~~
composer	exhibition	playwright	

B Personally speaking

Have you seen any good films recently? What's your taste in paintings? Are you reading anything at the moment? Who's your favourite singer? Write about yourself.

> At the moment I'm reading 'The Grapes of Wrath', by John Steinbeck. It's about an American family who have to leave their farm and go to California looking for work.

> Last week I went to see 'Metropolis', which is an old science fiction film about a city in the future. It was very good.

> Hank Wangford is a country and western singer. I like his music very much and I've got three of his records.

....
....
....
....
....
....
....
....
....

New words

Use this space to write down new words from the unit, with your own notes and examples.

TRANSLATION

Translate into your own language:

1 Picasso was born in Spain, but he painted most of his best-known pictures in France.

....

....

....

2 What's this poem about? I don't understand it.

....

....

3 Jaws III is on at the cinema tonight. Shall we go and see it together?

....

....

4 I like this music. I find it very relaxing.

....

....

Now cover up the left-hand side, and translate your sentences back into English.

LISTENING: Choosing a painting

You will hear someone talking about the pictures in Classroom Book, page 108–9:

A *Street Scene*
B *Woman's Head with Sombrero*
C *Painting 1937*
D *Landschaft am Meer*
E *Circus Girl*
F *Icarus*

1 Here are some of the comments he makes:

– I'd find it rather disturbing
– It's a very warm painting
– Suitable for a hall
– Interesting for a few moments
– I'd grow bored with it rather quickly
– A very peaceful painting

Which pictures do you think each comment is about?

2 Listen and decide which pictures he would put on a wall in his home. (Write ✔, ✗ or ? in the table.)
Add the comments above in their correct places.

	✔, ✗ or ?	Comment
A		
B		
C		
D		
E		
F		

3 Which painting is the man's favourite? ....

SOUND AND SPELLING: Words with *th*

1 Listen to these words on the tape.

/θ/: thick, thought, three, thing
/θ/: author, athletics, death, path, fifth, south, bath

/ð/: this, them, then, therefore
/ð/: other, father, southern, either, bathe

2 How do you say these words? Mark them /θ/ or /ð/. Then listen to the tape.

	earth		thumb
	theirs		mouth
	brother		these
	months		neither
	northern		breathe
	leather		cloth
	both		clothes

3 You will hear six sentences. Write down any words you hear with *th* in them.

DICTATION

You will hear part of the story *The Night in the Hotel* (Classroom Book, page 110, line 30 to line 35).

Listen and write down what you hear.

WRITING SKILLS: Sequence (3)

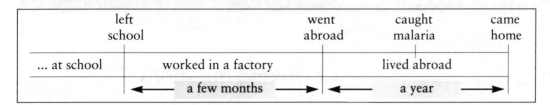

	left school		went abroad	caught malaria	came home
... at school	worked in a factory		lived abroad		
	← a few months →		← a year →		

1 The sentences below show different ways of organising information from the table above:

A He left school, **and then** got a job in a factory.
  After leaving | school, he worked in a factory for a few months.
  After he left |

B He went abroad for a year. But **before that** he worked in a factory to earn some money.
  Before | he went / going | abroad, he worked in a factory to earn some money.

C He left school, and a few months **later** he went abroad.
  A few months **after** leaving school, he went abroad.

D **While** | he was living / living | abroad, he caught malaria and nearly died.

2 Correct the mistakes in these sentences:

  a A few weeks after that he bought a new motorbike, he was injured in a road accident.
  b She moved to Buenos Aires to work as a sculptor. Two years after, she had her first exhibition.
  c Before to leave the house, I checked that all the lights were switched off.
  d Two years after he joining the firm, he was promoted to manager.
  e While staying in India. She visited the Taj Mahal several times.

3 Join these sentences to make a coherent story. Make any changes you think are necessary.

She said goodbye to her friends.	....
She went back to the hotel.	....
Fortunately there was no-one at the desk.	....
She quickly took the key for Room 24.	....
She took the lift to the second floor.	....
She put her ear to the keyhole and listened carefully.	....
She opened the door.	....
She slipped quietly into the room.	....
She switched the light on.	....
She found what she was looking for.	....
The book was in the wardrobe, under some shirts.	....
She looked quickly through it.	....
She put the book back in the wardrobe.	....
She left the room.	....

1 Verb forms

Write the correct form of the verbs.
Example:
They *'ve been* (be) married for 10 years.

1 We .... (spend) most of yesterday evening .... (play) cards.

2 He .... (stand) by the swimming pool when someone .... (come) up behind him and .... (push) him into the water.

3 She .... (play) for years, so I expect she .... (win) the match tomorrow.

4 Unless you .... (leave) me alone, I .... (call) the police.

5 I saw a little girl .... (sit) on the floor .... (play) with some wooden bricks. She .... (sing) to herself.

6 Oh dear! I think I .... (be) sick.

2 Asking questions

Complete the questions.
Example:
– How long *has he been* here?
– Not long. He arrived a few minutes ago.

1 – How much ....?
   – They'll pay you $20 an hour.

2 – How much .... that jacket?
   – Since Christmas. My sister gave it to me.

3 – What ....?
   – He's quite short and he wears glasses.

4 – I was talking to Ali just now.
   – Oh yes? What ....
     about?

5 – What .... in
     Malaysia?
   – It's hot and humid, and it rains quite a lot.

6 – How long ....
     private lessons?
   – Oh, for about a year now.

7 – What .... that
     picture?
   – I like it. The colours are beautiful.

3 Prepositions

Fill the gaps with prepositions from the box.

along	from	since	for
at	in	to	on
by	of	through	until

1 I was driving .... the road when I saw an old friend standing .... the bus stop.

2 She isn't very old – I think she's still .... her fifties.

3 When you arrive .... the airport you'll have to go .... customs.

4 It usually rains .... the coast, but it stays dry .... the mountains.

5 – I've been waiting .... nearly an hour.
   – That's nothing. I've been here .... 9 o'clock this morning.

6 He works .... 8 in the morning .... 6 in the evening, and then he goes .... an evening class.

7 The picture .... the woman's face is .... Picasso.

4 Word order

Put these jumbled sentences in the right order. Remember to begin each
sentence with a capital letter.

Example:

time of television a they watching lot spend .
They spend a lot of time watching television.

1 lunch they arrived telegram having the were while .

....

2 hair a dark with woman long tall she's .

....

3 home it to long take will how get ?

....

4 old 25 about is her years brother .

....

5 early is visit time the the Scotland to best summer .

....

6 hurry you ticket don't get if a might you not .

....

5 Writing paragraphs

Write a short paragraph (2 or 3 sentences) on the following:

1 Describe a past or present leader of your country.

....

....

....

2 Write about a favourite picture or book. Say why you like it.

....

....

....

3 How much time do you spend watching TV? What kind of programmes do you watch?

....

....

....

4 What do you think will happen in the world next week? Make three predictions.

....

....

....

Tapescripts

Unit 1 Asking for help

Conversation 1

A Excuse me. Er, excuse me, I'm looking for a large bookshop. I've – there is a particular book that I want and I've been into one or two bookshops already, and they don't have it. Perhaps you could tell me where the main bookshop in the town is.

B Yes, I can, and it's a very good one, and it's big. You go up this hill, you continue up there right to the top of the hill (*Yes.*) and it's on the right-hand side. It's called the Green Dragon Bookshop. (*The Green Dragon Bookshop.*) I'm sure they can help you.

A Thank you very much.

Conversation 2

A Oh excuse me. (*Yes.*) Um, could you tell me where I could get a good cheap meal, please?

B Oh yes, I think so. Do you know where the railway station is? (*Er, yes.*) Well if you go there you'll see a very nice little restaurant opposite the railway station. It's good basic English food – fish, chips, eggs, bacon – and it's lovely, really cheap.

A Not too expensive? (*No, no.*) Good. Thank you.

Conversation 3

A Excuse me, please (*Yes.*) I wonder if you could recommend a good hotel?

B Yes, um a very nice, cheap clean hotel (*Yes.*) is on the main road out of town, (*Yes.*) and it's on the right hand side, (*M-hm.*) it's um a white building

A And do you know the name?

B Yes, it's called Eden Court.

A Eden Court Hotel. Thank you.

Unit 2 Relatives

1 The oldest member of my family is my grandmother, and she is 104, believe it or not. She lives in Canada, she moved there years ago, about 70 years ago, and although she's nearly blind she's very active and very interested in life. She looks much younger than she is, because she wears a beautiful white wig.

2 Do you know, the most interesting member of my family is my brother. He's five years older than me, and he's an airline pilot, and he flies all over the world, goes to some really interesting places. At the moment he's flying to Australia and back. I get on with him really well – I feel I have quite a boring job compared with him.

3 The nicest member of my family is my Uncle Bob. He's not very rich, but he is very very generous. And he sends me presents for my birthday and at Christmas, which are always a lovely surprise, and sometimes he sends presents when it isn't my birthday at all. And I'm always very pleased to see him.

4 The poorest member of my family is my grandmother. She used to be quite wealthy, but her husband, my grandfather, spent all the money and then died and she was left with nothing. Now she lives in a very small flat, won't have any money from our family, and she's really very poor.

Unit 3 Japanese New Year

A few days before the New Year, housewives start cooking special food for New Year's Day and on the New Year's Eve the whole of household, every household do a big cleaning up. The idea is to get rid of the dirt of the past year, and welcome the new. When the family's finished cleaning the house, they sit round and start watching television or start getting ready for New Year's – New Year's Day meal, which is the first meal of the year. Then the Japanese television or radio broadcast 108 bells. And then this 108th bell is supposed to be ringing just (a) fraction before the midnight, so you can imagine how important the timing is. Now as soon that 108th bell is rung, we all say 'Happy New Year' and some families put special kimonos on, or special dress on, to go to, to visit their shrine, and we come home and eat the special New Year's Day's food, which had been prepared by housewives previously, and we drink lots of rice wine, and we just sort of celebrate amongst the family.

Unit 4 Likes and dislikes

1 I'm not sure about planes. I don't like it when they take off – I get very frightened, I have to hold somebody's hand. Once they're up in the air then I don't mind so much, except that I get a little bored.

2 What I like about the train is that when you're sitting on it you really can't do anything else, so it's a perfect opportunity to read a book.

3 I use public transport mostly I suppose just to get me from A to B. And I get very bored – usually you can't even sit down, and it takes forever to get somewhere.

4 Without any doubt I use the car the most, and I think I probably enjoy it the most because I find it very convenient. I can listen to music in it, I can listen to the radio, and I can get from A to B exactly in quite a fast time.

Unit 5 These days

1 We've got a family of friends coming to stay with us tonight and for the rest of the weekend, and at the moment we're moving mattresses about the place because we haven't got enough beds for them all. There'll be eight of us altogether, no nine. And one of my children has got 'flu so nobody can sleep in his room. So they'll be sleeping in the sitting room and the dining room and on the landing. So we're as I say moving mattresses about, um – we're looking for a new house at the moment because we just don't find ours big enough if we're going to have people to stay all the time.

2 Well, at the moment I'm working really hard for my exams – they're in about three months' time, so most of the reading I'm doing at the moment is for my exams. I'm really looking forward to reading a good novel when the exams are over. And then I'm going to start looking for a job, and I really don't know what will happen then.

Unit 6 Polish dishes

A What have we got to eat here?

B Well, this is a dish called *bigos*. All you need to make bigos is sweet cabbage and a sour cabbage, and some pieces of cooked meat – different ones, whatever you have at hand, really. And there is one thing you really have to have, which is smoked bacon. Then you just cook the cabbage, then you mix all those things together. You put a lot of spices, you can add some tomatoes, and you just stew it very slowly. And the more times you reheat it the better it, it is.

And this is *chlodnik*. This is a soup, which you make of young beetroots. You just chop young beetroots, including leaves, and you just cook it as an ordinary soup. Then you add some generous amount of cream, and you serve it cool with some boiled eggs, which is a perfect dish for a hot summer day.

Unit 7 When did you last...?

A – When did you last cook a meal?
  – Um, very recently, actually. I got in quite late last night, at about 10.30, and er cooked myself some fried eggs on toast and sausages, and ate it about half an hour later.
B – When did you last drink champagne?
  – Oh, I think the last time I drank champagne was at a friend's wedding about three months ago. And they had a party afterwards, and they served champagne.
C – When did you last go to the dentist?
  – I went to the dentist a couple of days ago, and he said that all of my teeth were in fine condition, so that I needed no work done. I was very happy.
D – When did you last sing a song in public?
  – Well, it was last Friday, after I'd been to a friend's party, and it was out in the street, actually. I sang this song in public because I think I'd had a very good time at the party.

Unit 8 Favourite rooms

1 My favourite room is the one where I play my music. I play the music quite loud in there. I've got very big loudspeakers, and it's a good room for that because it's quite big – I can get quite a long way back from the speakers to listen to the music. But with it being big the problem with it it's very cold most of the time, I can never get it warm enough. And another thing that's wrong with it really is that there's a very big window, and in the summer I like to open the window, and then all the neighbours complain about the music.
2 My favourite room at the moment is my daughter's bedroom, which is the biggest room in the house, and is full of all sorts of things that she loves very dearly and I'm not allowed to touch. She has a very nice wooden bed and some wooden furniture in the room, and there's a shelf all the way round it, and it is full of soft toys, that she has collected for 15 years. It's got a dear little window, which I like very much, but it's so full of things that I can't clean it, and that annoys me.

Unit 9 Panel discussion

P And now on to the next topic, and we're going to ask our guests for their opinions about news programmes. Are they any good? Do you think there are too many or too few? Do the current news programmes focus on the right things? Steve.

1 Well, I certainly think that there are, there are enough news programmes every day, but er I've always been of the opinion that it's far too local, they focus on events that are just going on in this country. There are more important international issues, such as you know there are wars going on, there are famines, that often aren't even mentioned in news … (*Oh no, oh no.*) You don't agree?
2 Oh yes , I, I agree with that, but I'm amazed that you think there are enough news programmes. How can you have enough news programmes? I think the more the better, really. Some countries after all have a 24 hour news channel…
3 I don't watch it at all, it's too depressing. The only thing I watch is the local news. That's what people want to know. People don't want to know that the world's about to end and about all the disasters. I just don't watch the news, it's always bad news … (*I disagree with that, I think …*)

Unit 10 Working clothes

1 Well, because I don't have to go into an office or anything I work at home, um I just wear comfortable clothes. Er, jeans, sometimes a tracksuit, something like that. I suppose if I'm meeting a, a client and having to put on a bit of a show I'll wear a jacket, but er I never really wear a tie, sometimes a, a polo neck shirt or something but, no I don't dress up much, I'm afraid.
2 Well, because I work for a solicitor um and I meet clients, I have to dress you know very, I have to dress up at work, and er people expect me to wear fairly formal sort of suits, um I can wear a skirt and blouse, er but um very rarely do I wear trousers, and certainly I couldn't wear jeans in that sort of situation.
3 Being a writer I'm working from home. I can really wear exactly what I feel like, jeans or shorts in summer and blouses, anything, T-shirts. Of course, if I've got to go and see a publisher and try and interest them I do try and dress a little bit more smartly, I'll put on better trousers or a dress or something.
4 Well, I work in an office, so I don't have very much choice in what I wear. I have three suits, I have a dark blue suit, a black suit and a dark grey suit, and I wear one of those every day. I have one pair of very nice black brogue shoes which luckily goes with all three suits, so I wear those. And I have a rather nice light grey sleeveless pullover which if it's a chilly day I may wear underneath my suits.

Unit 11 Two journeys

A Right well, because we've come into some money quite unexpectedly, I think we'll probably take the Orient Express across France through Switzerland to Venice. And we're going to spend two or three days in Venice, which is a marvellous city. We'll visit all the tourist sights of the city, there are some marvellous restaurants there, which we will probably visit. And then we're going to hire a car and go to Florence, Pisa, down to Rome, and back up to Venice again. That should take us about nine days. Then we will probably spend one more night in Venice, and take Concorde back to London.
B We're going to go from London, across the Channel on the ferry, and catch a train to Paris. And I expect we'll spend, ooh a couple of days in Paris – we're taking tents, so we're planning to do a bit of camping. And then we'll probably hitch down to the south of France, well, I expect we'll do a bit of swimming, lying on the beach. And then if we've got time, we're going to cross the border and go to Spain, and visit Barcelona, I expect. And we'll stay there for a few days. And then we'll probably – well I don't know what we're going to do. We'll have to get back somehow, maybe catch a train.

Unit 12 Feeling ill

Last week at work, I was, I was sitting at my desk working at my computer when suddenly I felt rather ill, and I felt very hot and I had a nasty headache and my eyes were hurting a lot. So I telephoned and made an appointment to see the doctor. And that evening I went along to the doctor's, and he asked me a lot of questions and he asked me to take my shirt off and he examined me. He listened to my chest, he looked in my eyes and he looked in my ears. And at the end he said, 'Well, you've got 'flu.' And he wrote me out a prescription for some medicine, and told me to go home, to take the medicine three times a day and to stay in bed for a few days. So on the way home I went to the chemist's and I picked up the medicine. Um, and just as the doctor told me I went to bed, I took the medicine three times a day, and I stayed in bed for two or three days and slept. And sure enough, after that I felt much better and I was able to go back to work. But the funny thing is I don't think I got better because of the medicine at all. I think I got better just because I had a three-day break from working with my computers.

Unit 13 The most and the least

1 A Well, I don't think I'm all that musical, um but I play cello, saxophone, banjo, recorder and flute, um as well as a little guitar, so I enjoy playing a lot and love singing as well.
  B When I was a young boy I played the piano for a few years, but I gave it up when I was about eleven and – Well, I've not played a musical instrument since.
  C I learnt to play the piano when I was at school, and also the recorder. I carried on playing the piano for quite a while, but then stopped, sadly, but I have always sung in, in – I've always enjoyed singing.
2 A I'm afraid I only speak English, and a little school French, 'O' level French – um I only really speak, speak English.
  B I've got a Spanish father and as a boy I learnt both Spanish and English. I also can speak French quite well and Italian, and I'm not bad at German either.
  C I learnt French and German at school, but wasn't very good, but good enough to be able to go to France or Germany and get by and be able to have a conversation.
3 A Oh, I've travelled a lot – um I've been to most of the countries in Europe, um I've also been to Canada and at the same time went to the United States of America, and also down to Mexico, which was lovely.
  B I'm sorry to say I've never ever been outside Britain. I must do it sometime.
  C I've been very lucky, because my parents worked for one of the airlines, and I've been able to travel. I've travelled to Australia and to Japan, and last year we went to China.

Unit 14 Living in London

1 Well, I like living in London, mainly because I live right in the centre. If I want to go to a theatre, I can leave my house about 15 minutes before the show starts, and walk to the theatre. I can do the same with a cinema. In the morning, I can get up, I can go into Soho and buy fresh croissants and coffee – and generally there is a wonderful cosmopolitan air about the whole place.
2 I don't like living in London at all. We've got a very small garden with a railway at the bottom, so it's noisy. Aeroplanes go over every two minutes, so you can't sit outside because there are trains and planes, and it's very dirty as well. My journey to work is horrendous, because I get into a packed tube, it's packed with people. We never get a seat, people are extremely rude and push in front of you to get a seat, and the same returning home in the evenings. I think living out in the country must be much nicer.

Unit 15 Have you ever...?

1 I've only ever been sailing once, and that was on my ninth birthday, when my brother took his girlfriend out in her boat very late at night – it must have been eleven or twelve – and I was allowed out specially because it was my birthday. And I was allowed to take a fishing line with me and trail it over the side and I actually caught a fish.
2 No, I haven't acted in a play, but I was in an opera. I was one of the people on stage who had to do things. Not sing, because I can't sing that well but I just had to be there and do things. But it was good fun – I really enjoyed it.
3 Yes, I have. When I was 16 my brother had a motorbike and I wanted to have a go on it. And he put me on and started me off, but unfortunately he didn't tell me how to stop, and I went round this square about four times, and each time he shouted out to me. And in the end he managed to tell me. But I was quite frightened.
4 Yes, last week in fact. We went to see Hamlet at the Old Vic, and it was marvellous.
5 No, I haven't. I think to go into a casino you need lots of money, and you need to have a streak in you that wants to lose that money or win it or whatever it is that makes you want to go into a casino, I don't have it.

Unit 16 Rock climbing

A Once I had tried rock climbing, I decided that I really liked it myself quite a lot, because it wasn't a strenuous sport, it wasn't like an endurance sport, not like walking in the hills – that you just have to keep plodding on – but rock climbing was fast and exciting, and funnily enough it's not so much like a sport, it's more like problem solving – that I think is the interesting thing. And even something which is small, a little boulder that's maybe 12 feet high, and doesn't look in any way unusual or difficult, can still present you with a lot of problems, and you can get very absorbed in trying to make your, find a way to make yourself move up instead of just over or stay still, and so in that sense it's an unusual sport, I think.
B What's been the most exciting thing that's happened to you in rock climbing?
A The most scary incident was actually coming off a rock in a place in Italy where I was climbing, and it wasn't terribly steep, so instead of falling free on the rope and being stopped, which happens so fast that you are really hardly aware of – you don't have time to be frightened. In this case, because it was a more sloping mountainside, I actually was bouncing and slithering all the way down, and I kept thinking 'I'm going to hurt myself, I'm definitely going to hurt myself, if I hit another time I'm going to hurt myself, I'm going break my arm, I'm going to break my leg,' and I had plenty of time to have all these bad thoughts, and be very scared indeed, and think 'Oh suppose the rope breaks or doesn't hold.'

Unit 17 Radio phone-in

A And we have Susan on the phone, who's phoning us from Woking. Susan, can you hear?
B Yes, I can. Hello.
A Hello. Um, Susan, what's your problem?
B Well, you see the thing is, I have a very good relationship with my husband, we've been married about five years now, but a few months ago he got a new job. And he works very hard, and when he comes home in the evening he's exhausted, and all he wants to do is sit in front of the telly and go to sleep. (*I see.*) Well, I work too, but what I want to do in the evenings is go out and have some fun and relax a bit, and you know he won't come with me, he really won't, and – I just don't know what to do.
A Chris, have you got any ideas how we can help Susan?
C Yes. Susan, I would suggest you actually talk to him about the problem. Talk to him – see if you can get him to come out with you shall we say for a couple of nights in the week, and then you perhaps stay at home watching the telly for the other couple of ... compromise, that's the thing – work at it and compromise.
D Um, Susan, if I can come in here. What I would suggest is – I don't know if you've tried this, but maybe you arrange to go out with some friends on your own, you know, some girlfriends or something, to the cinema, say. If he wants to stay at home, that's fine, but I don't think you should let him stop you from doing what you want.
A There you are, Susan – I hope that's helped you, and from all of us here we very much hope that you sort things out quickly. OK, we're moving on now to Sharon, who's calling us from...

Unit 18 A security guard

1 A Can you tell me what sort of work do you do?
  B Yes, I'm a Securicor guard.
  A I see. What does that involve?
  B Well, er Securicor guards are hired by companies to guard their buildings during the day and sometimes during the night, and that's precisely what we do. Our job is to prevent people from breaking into these buildings , and to look after all aspects of security, really.

2 A What particular aspects about the job do you enjoy?
  B Um, well it's, there's a certain amount of variety, you don't always work in the same place, so you travel a little bit. The people are very friendly, um..
  A Anything you don't like about it?
  B Oh, quite a lot, yes. The pay's not very good, it can be very boring, and you have to work very long hours.
  A So you don't get much free time?
  B That's right. Not if you want to earn overtime, which is really how you earn a decent wage.
  A And what would be a decent wage?
  B Well, in order to earn say £150 a week you have to work, ooh a good 70, 80 hours a week.
  A It's a long week.
  B It is, yes, yes.

Unit 19 Two stories

A I had a very embarrassing experience recently. I went to a friend's wedding, and it all went very successfully, and they had a video made of the wedding and the party – the reception afterwards. And a few weeks later they invited us round to go and watch the video, because it had, it had just arrived. So we went round, and there we were watching the video of the wedding and the reception, and at one point we suddenly noticed the father of the groom stealing the wallet out of a coat in a cloakroom, and it was very clear to see so it was extremely embarrassing, and I didn't know what to do or say really. In the end, I just had to pretend that I hadn't seen anything.

B This happened to me a few years ago now on the Underground in London. And it was a Saturday and I was going to do some shopping, and the carriage that I was in was full of football supporters. They were all quite young, I mean they weren't, they weren't men, they were boys, they were I would think 13, 14, something like that. And first of all there was just a lot of noise, and then they started rocking the carriage of the train. And it was absolutely terrifying. The train was very full by this time and I don't like crowded places anyway, but the rocking and the noise were really very very frightening indeed. And eventually the doors of the train opened, and I got out – I could hardly stand up – and got onto the platform and just collapsed in tears on a seat. It was awful – even now thinking about it I get quite shaky and frightened – it was horrible.

Unit 20 Famous people

1 This person usually wore black. She er, I remember that – her always as being old, but she was only old because she lived to a very old age. When she was young she was very pretty, but the picture we have of her, I think, is of somebody very old, dressed all in black, with a sort of – the hair tied in a tight bun, and she didn't often laugh.

2 He was a short man, who had been very elegant and always wore a uniform which was white trousers, tight white trousers and a short blue jacket with gold embroidery. He also wore boots, he had dark hair, and dark eyes. His nose was pointed, and he had a small mouth and quite a pointed chin, which made him look as though he was listening all the time. He also wore a hat, usually, a three-pointed hat.

3 She was quite a tall woman and she had a very striking face, quite an angular face. She was dark-skinned, and she had greying hair – it became more grey as the time went by. A very peaceful looking person, and a very impressive looking woman. Very striking indeed, and in fact I think as she got older she became more striking.

Unit 21 Driving test

Well, you come out of the main driving test centre and your instructor will ask you where your car is, and to take him to your car. So you walk up to it, get in, put your safety belt on, and the instructor gets in the other side. And he normally has a clipboard with various bits of paper and he starts to make little ticks and crosses even as early on in the test as that, and you're thinking to yourself 'Have I done something wrong already?' Then he'll ask you to drive, drive off. You'll drive along the road, then the instructor will ask you to turn left or right, ask you what motoring sign you've just passed and you have to tell him, then he'll ask you to do perhaps an emergency stop, pretending that a child has run into the road and you must put your foot down on the brake really quickly, and then drive on. He'll be looking to see that you're confident in the car. You find out if you've passed at the end of perhaps an hour-long test. He'll ask you to drive back into the car park at the, of the test centre, and you'll stop and think 'What is he going to say? Have I passed or failed?' And he takes out a bit of paper, and if it's pink you've failed, if it's green you've passed.

Unit 22 Living in a hot climate

I think the hottest place I've ever lived in is Kuwait, in the Arabian Gulf. It's certainly very hot most of the year, but particularly in July and August of course – it can reach up to 53 degrees centigrade in, in late July. It's a dry heat rather than a humid one though, so you're not as hot as you would be say in England perhaps if it reached 50 degrees. And of course everything is air-conditioned, so you're hardly ever out in it when it's as hot as that. The cars are air-conditioned, the schools are air-conditioned, every office is air-conditioned, your houses are air-conditioned, so you just basically just drive to a place with your a/c on in the car, leap out, run into your school or your office, stay there all day, usually having to put a jacket on 'cause it's often really quite cool inside, then you jump back into your car again and drive home. Uh, the water's often too hot to swim in, the sea water that is, during the summer. It's usually too hot even to sunbathe in the middle of summer – you just feel that your skin is sizzling.

Unit 23 24 hours

A Mary, er last Friday. Do you remember how much time you spent working?
B Well, I was spring cleaning at home actually, and it just seems to go on and on. I suppose about six hours actually.
A Um and what about travel?
B Well, travel's funny I suppose going to the shops, does that count? I, I do that quite often, I sometimes go twice or maybe three times a day. The shops are just at the top of the road. So, I suppose I spend about, mm a couple of hours travelling.
A Um, meals, what about eating?
B Eating, hmm, don't get much chance for that really. I have a little boy, you know, and er eating's very er haphazard. I suppose I spend two quarter of an hours, lunchtime and teatime, and then I have an evening meal. Sometimes the evening meal's a bit more leisurely. I suppose about an hour and a half really.
A How much time do you think you spent talking to people on Friday?
B Well, as I say it's really just going to the shops. I, I talk to the shopkeepers a lot. Oh, I suppose an

hour, an hour talking.

A What about reading?

B Oh, well I don't get much chance to read myself, but I read to my little boy a lot. Um, that can be about three hours a day.

A Do you watch TV at all?

B Well, I like to, but of course I, I fall asleep at the end of the day. There are certain programmes I like to watch. I'd say about two hours.

A And finally, what about sleep?

B Huh, I like sleep. Oh, about five hours a night. Quite often it's broken sleep.

Unit 24 Choosing a painting

I'd certainly choose this one here with the landscape, with the sea in the background. I find that one particularly attractive. It's a very warm painting, I think. And I'd also take the portrait of the young girl, the darker one, which is a very peaceful painting, I think. I'm not so sure about the other portrait, the – with very bright colours. I would find that perhaps rather disturbing to have on a wall. The street scene, I don't know – it's interesting for a few moments but perhaps not for a long time. The strange figure with the red heart, I think, yes I think I'd like that one but maybe not in a room, perhaps in a hall for looking at as I walked past it, maybe. And the abstract painting with the shapes, I don't think I'd have that one, no, I think I'd grow bored with that one rather quickly.

The one I like best is the head and shoulders of the young woman. She's such a peaceful looking person, I think. And although the colours are not very startling, they're very gentle, and I feel really that it's a very relaxing picture to look at.

Answer key

Unit 1 Description

A There is(n't) & There are(n't)

1 There's; there aren't
2 Is there; there isn't; there are
3 There aren't; there's; there are
4 Are there; there's

B Have got

1 The village has got a post office.
2 Has this car got an ashtray?
3 The bathroom hasn't got a window.
4 The zoo hasn't got any lions.
5 Have the classrooms got carpets?
6 My office has got central heating.

C Two descriptions

Possible answers:

1 In the reception area there's a low table and there are some armchairs. There's a telephone on the wall. There's a lift.
2 The bedroom's got a television and a desk. On the wall above the desk there's a picture. There's a shower next to the desk.

D Place prepositions

1 opposite		6 behind	
2 in		7 below	
3 above		8 near	
4 next		9 between	
5 front		10 convenient	

Listening: Asking for help

1 bookshop; the hill; right hand; Green; Bookshop
2 *a* restaurant; ④ on the map
  b cheap; small; English
  c fish; chips; eggs; bacon
3 *a* hotel
  b F; T; F; T; T

Pronunciation: Where's the stress

2 office   information
  computer   furniture
  hotel   hungry
  opposite   beside
  café   understand
3 *b* I want to post a letter.
  c Where's the bathroom?
  d There's a policeman at the door.
  e Are you a student here?
  f How much food have we got?

Dictation

1 It's a beautiful place, and it's got some lovely beaches. Unfortunately, it's a bit quiet in the evenings.
2 It hasn't got a language lab, but there's a video and there are cassette players in all the classrooms.
3 I have to share my room with two other people, and there's only one bathroom on each floor.

Reading: Islands

1 Stromboli
2 *c* Stromboli   *g* Stromboli
  d Herm   *h* Herm
  e Herm, Stromboli   *i* Herm
  f Herm   *j* Stromboli
3 – Herm: beaches
  – Stromboli: a volcano

Unit 2 Family and friends

A Family tree

1 grandfather	11 sister
2 grandmother	12 brother-in-law
3 aunt	13 nephew
4 uncle	14 niece
5 mother	15 daughter-in-law
6 father	16 son
7 mother-in-law	17 daughter
8 father-in-law	18 son-in-law
9 sister-in-law	19 grandson
10 brother	20 granddaughter

Not used: cousin

B Relationships

1 goes out with   4 pregnant
2 get divorced   5 engaged; get married
3 married; single   6 divorced

Listening: Relatives

1 104 years old; lives in Canada; very interested in life; nearly blind; wears a wig
2 five years older than me; an airline pilot; goes to interesting places
3 not very rich; very generous; often sends me presents
4 lives in a small flat; very poor; used to be rich

Sound and spelling: Words with *a*

2 B name	A happy	B day	A catch
D small	B train	D warm	D talk
C faster	C hard	B station	E what

3 I went to the station to catch a train.
What's the man's name?
It was a warm autumn day.
The waiter came to the table.

Dictation

John and Mary meet at a party. A friend introduces them. He invites her out to see a film, and afterwards they have dinner together. They start going out together regularly. They decide to get engaged, and he buys her a diamond ring. They get married, and invite all their friends and relations to the wedding. They fly off to the Caribbean for their honeymoon.

Writing skills: Sentences

1 Five
2 I have no brothers or sisters, but I have two cousins. One of them is younger than me, and the other is older. The younger one is 19 and has just started university. The older one is married and lives with her family in Australia.
3 *Possible answer:*
I have one sister. She is older than me, and is studying to be a doctor. My father is a shopkeeper, and has two sisters. One is retired and lives in Scotland. The other lives in London and works in a children's hospital.

Unit 3 Habits, customs and facts

A Simple verbs

Across: 1 watches 6 do 7 give 8 reads 9 ask
11 flies 13 have 14 spend 16 does 17 look at
Down: 1 work 2 teaches 3 has 4 sell 5 begins
7 goes 10 send 11 feel 12 speak 15 go

B Do(es)(n't)

1 Does; doesn't; don't
2 does
3 Do; don't; doesn't
4 does; Do; do; do; doesn't

C Asking Wh- questions

1 Where does she park her car?
2 What do crocodiles eat?
3 What time (*or* When) do you have lunch?
4 How do you want to pay?
5 Why does he walk to work?
6 When (*or* Where) do you use your English?

D Frequency

Possible answers:
1 It doesn't rain very often in California.
2 The sun always rises in the east.
3 Businessmen usually wear suits.
4 Siberia is always cold in winter.
5 People don't usually wear sweaters in bed.
6 Students don't often go to sleep in class.

Listening: Japanese New Year

6; 2; 4; 1; 8; 7; 5; 9; 3

Pronunciation: The sound /ə/

3 a woman   breakfast
   an actor   never
   grandfather   the winter
4 b In the summer he works in a factory.
   c Does she read a newspaper?
   d I never visit my relations.
   e The town centre is busy today.

Dictation

Many hotels serve what they call 'full English breakfast'. First they bring you cereal and fruit juice, then you get egg, bacon and tomato, and then toast and marmalade. In fact, few people in Britain eat such a big breakfast. It's more normal to have just one of these things, with a cup of tea or coffee. Nowadays, a lot of people start the day with muesli or yoghurt.

Reading: Reptiles and amphibians

1 crocodile   4 sea snake
2 chameleon   5 bullfrog
3 turtle   *(The gecko is not described.)*

Unit 4 Going places

A Public opinions

1 uncomfortable   5 dangerous
2 expensive   6 slow
3 reliable   7 unreliable
4 crowded   8 cheap

B Rail, road and air

1 office	8 stop	15 takes
2 return	9 fill	16 passengers
3 station	10 catch	17 airport
4 time	11 bicycle	18 belts
5 platform	12 driver	19 flight
6 train	13 petrol	20 check
7 seat	14 off *or* out	21 steward

You can use rail, road and air to get from one place to another.

Listening: Likes and dislikes

P I get very frightened.
B It takes forever to get somewhere.
P I don't like it when they take off.
C I find it very convenient.
C I can listen to the radio.
T It's a perfect opportunity to read a book.
B Usually you can't even sit down.
B I get very bored.
C I can get from A to B exactly.
P I have to hold somebody's hand.

Sound and spelling: words with *e*

2 D few B sleep
   A yellow A dress
   C earn C early
   A ready E horses
   B jeans E market
   E beside A forget

3 Don't forget to go to bed early.
   I wore jeans and she wore her new yellow dress.
   They sell meat and cheese at the market.
   I waited a few weeks for her letter.

Dictation

I usually go by train, because it's only a bit slower than the plane and it's more reliable. It's about $100 return. The journey takes about four hours. I usually catch the 10.30 train, which reaches New York at ten past two. It's comfortable, and it's always on time.

Writing skills: Punctuation

2 Ernest Hemingway
   German
   the Oxford School of English
   October
   the Alps
   London
   Tuesday
   Can I go now?
3 *a* He speaks German but not Italian.
   b Does this train go to Moscow?
   c The meeting will be on Friday, 14th May.
   d Can I get there by bus?
4 My sister has got a new bike and she spends nearly all her time on it. Every afternoon she comes home from school and quickly has something to eat. Then she goes out on her bike and cycles round the streets until it gets dark. I never see her at weekends because she spends all day riding her bike. In the evenings she reads magazines about cycling. It's her birthday next week. Do you know what I'm going to give her? I'm going to give her a mirror for her bike.

Unit 5 Now

A Cross -ing words

Across: 2 going 4 playing 7 having 9 winning 11 changing 12 making 13 running
Down: 1 doing 3 lying 5 living 6 shining 8 ringing 10 talking 11 coming

B Simple or continuous?

1 is ('s) wearing
2 is ('s) washing
3 stay; are ('re) staying
4 is ('s) having
5 washes
6 teaches
7 is ('s) writing
8 wear
9 am ('m) teaching
10 have
11 write

C Asking Wh- questions

1 Where are they staying?
2 Who is she talking to?
3 Why is the baby crying?
4 What are you reading?
5 How are you feeling?
6 How many rings is she wearing?

D There is/are + -ing

1 There are some people in the kitchen eating.
   (*or* There are some people eating in the kitchen.)
2 There are two children sitting on the stairs.
3 There's a woman playing the piano.
4 There are two people dancing on a table.
5 There are some people outside trying to get in.
6 There's a disc jockey playing loud music.

Listening: These days

1 woman and man 5 woman
2 man 6 woman
3 woman 7 woman
4 neither 8 neither

Pronunciation: Reduced vowels (1)

2 *a* He's looking *for* a job.
   b She's got lots *of* friends.
   c It's twenty *to* three.
   d I'd like fish *and* chips, please.
   e Don't give *them* any money.
   f Are there any letters *for* me?
   g You need *some* new clothes.
   h You aren't listening *to* me.
   i I got it *from* the library.
   j This is a photo *of* my parents.
   k Sorry, I'm busy *at* the moment.
   l *And* then we all went home.

Dictation

1 I don't watch television, but I read a lot in the evenings. At the moment I'm reading a novel by Doris Lessing, called 'The Golden Notebook'.
2 It's really boring here at the moment. Everyone's away, so I'm not doing much. I'm just sitting around reading and watching TV.
3 I usually read a lot, but just now I'm not reading anything. I'm far too busy. I'm working overtime every night.

Reading: What's going on?

1A, 2B, 3A, 4C, 5B, 6A, 7C, 8C, 9B, 10A, 11A, 12C, 13B, 14C

Unit 6 Food and drink

A Kinds of food

A 1 orange   5 banana   9 cucumber
   2 carrots   6 cabbage   10 potatoes
   3 apple   7 grapes   11 pear
   4 lemon   8 onion   12 greengrocer

B 1 cheese   5 butter   9 cake
   2 flour   6 milk   10 meat
   3 pepper   7 sugar   11 salt
   4 eggs   8 rice   12 supermarket

B Talking about food

1 kind of; need; cooked; served
2 serves; order; dish; bill; reserve
3 order; dish; made from; served

Listening: Polish dishes

1 *Bigos:* tomatoes; cabbage; meat; bacon; spices
   Chlodnik: beetroot; eggs; cream; beetroot leaves
2 chlodnik; chlodnik; bigos; chlodnik

Sound and spelling: Words with *i*

2 A drink   D field
   C shirt   B right
   A different   A swimming
   B write   B library
   C first   C bird
   B die   A with
3 Give me a piece of birthday cake.
   He always wears a white shirt and a tie.
   My sister likes swimming.
   They received tickets for the first night.

Dictation

A Good evening. Have you reserved a table?
B No, I'm afraid we haven't.
A What about this table by the window?
B Yes, that'll be fine, thanks.
A Are you ready to order now?
B Yes, I think so. I'll have the chicken, please.
A What would you like to drink?
B Just mineral water, please.
B That was a lovely meal. Could we have the bill please?

Writing skills: Reference

1 *b* John; the eggs
   c the men; the room
   d Rome; Rome
2 *a* it; there   *d* them; they
   b It; she; it   *e* there; her
   c him; he
3 A new restaurant opened in town last week, so I
decided to go there to see what it was like. After a few
minutes a waitress came over to the table and gave me
a menu, but she wasn't very friendly. I ordered
chicken and chips. Half an hour later, she brought the
food. It wasn't very good. The chicken was tough, and

it had a rather strange taste. The chips were even
worse; they were half cold and very greasy. I couldn't
eat them at all.
I called the waitress and asked her to bring me the
bill. It came to £25. I asked to see the manager. I told
him that I thought £25 was too much for such a bad
meal. I gave him £5, and then walked out of the
restaurant. I'll certainly never go there again.

Revision and extension Units 1–6

1 Verb forms

1 Are; am
2 haven't got
3 drives; 's got
4 lives; 's staying
5 'm studying; don't speak

2 Asking questions

1 How many children have they got?
2 What are you doing these days?
3 What time does he (usually) get home?
4 Where do you work?
5 Is there a bank near here?
6 Why are you wearing that heavy coat?
7 Do you smoke?

3 Prepositions

1 at the station
2 of me
3 between my room and theirs
4 to my birthday party
5 for breakfast
6 at home
7 to the airport; at 6.30
8 on time
9 at this table; by the window
10 by train
11 with that singer

4 Word order

1 There are some children swimming in the river.
2 Could we have the bill please?
3 Do you live near the town centre?
4 I usually listen to the news on the radio.
5 Have you got a shower in your bathroom?
6 They don't go to the cinema very often.
   or They don't very often go to the cinema.

Unit 7 The past

A Irregular squares

Top left: 1 swam   2 were   3 rode   4 made
Top right: 1 threw   2 had   3 went   4 drank
Bottom left: 1▶ was 1▼ wrote   2 slept   3 woke   4 left
Bottom right: 1 bought   2 sent   3 wore   4 gave
   5 caught   6 felt

B Positive and negative

1 Bella had a bath.
2 Dick didn't go to the shops.
3 Bella didn't make a cake.
4 Dick watched television.
5 Bella read the newspaper.
6 Dick lost his umbrella.
7 Bella didn't take the dog for a walk.
8 Bella drove to work.

C Asking Wh- questions

1 Where did they go last night?
2 Why did he leave?
3 How much (money) did you spend?
4 What did she say?
5 When did your mother arrive?
6 How did you get in?

D Time expressions

1 in 1941; at one o'clock; on January 1st; in February; in April; 50 years ago
2 ten years ago; last Tuesday
3 last week; on Monday; in the morning; at ten in the evening; on Wednesday; on Friday morning; yesterday morning
4 this morning; at 12.30; this afternoon; half an hour ago

Listening: When did you last ...?

1 B They had a party afterwards.
  C All my teeth were in fine condition
  A I ate it about half an hour later.
  D I'd had a very good time.
  A Fried eggs on toast.
  C I needed no work done.
  D I'd been to a friend's party.
  A I got in quite late.
  B At a friend's wedding.
  C I was very happy.
3 last night
  about three months ago
  a couple of days ago
  last Friday

Pronunciation: Reduced vowels (2)

a Where *can* I change some money?
b How *do* you spell 'pronunciation'?
c Those chocolates *were* very good.
d Where *are* they living these days?
e There *was* snow on the ground.
f What knid of car *does* she drive?
g He said he *was* very busy.
h Some ghosts *are* quite friendly.
i What part of Finland *do* you come from?
j I *was* born on Friday 13th.
k You *can* stay if you like.
l There *were* only two seats left.

Dictation

When Joseph Merlin invented roller skates in 1760, he decided to demonstrate them at a large party. Half way through the party, he came into the ballroom wearing his skates and playing a violin. Unfortunately he didn't know how to turn or stop, and he crashed into a large mirror at the end of the room. He broke the mirror and his violin, and ended up in hospital.

Reading: Jokes

1f; 2e; 3h; 4j; 5d

Unit 8 Somewhere to live

A Phrases

1 a view of the sea
2 the ninth floor
3 a detached house
4 faces north
5 a main road
6 looks out on a park
7 block of flats

B Furniture and fittings

1 coffee (table); dining (table)
2 sink; washbasin; bath; shower; toilet
3 fridge; cooker; lamp; light
4 chair; armchair; sofa; bed
5 carpet; curtains
6 desk
7 cupboard; wardrobe
8 mirror; bookshelves

C What are they like?

1 noisy   5 dark
2 sunny   6 bare
3 untidy   7 quiet
4 convenient   8 spacious

Listening: Favourite rooms

1 loud; stereo; big; difficult; big; often open; and then
2 1: my ~~sister's~~ daughter's bedroom
   2: is the ~~smallest~~ biggest room
   3: has a ~~metal~~ wooden bed
   4: and ~~no other~~ some wooden furniture
   5: shelf ~~beside the bed~~ all the way round
   6: full of ~~books~~ soft toys
   7: for ~~five~~ fifteen years
   8: a ~~big~~ little window
   9: which I ~~don't~~ like

Sound and spelling: Words with o (1)

2 B alone   A sorry
   A cottage   B boat
   B know   A bottle
   C another   D town
   C love   B broken
   D about   C month
3 My mother's in town doing some shopping.
   They live alone in a cottage in the mountains.
   Go and get another bottle of milk.
   My son's coming home next month.

Dictation

1 I've found a quiet little flat in the old part of the town. It's a bit small – just two rooms – but it's got a balcony which looks out on a square.
2 We've just moved to a house in the suburbs. It's got four bedrooms and a large garden. It's very spacious, and there's lots of room for the children. The living room faces south, so it's quite sunny.

Writing skills: Joining ideas

2 *a* but   *b* so   *c* but   *d* so   *e* and
3 A
4 *Possible answer:*
   I've just moved to a new flat. It has a living room, a bedroom and a small kitchen. It's near the town centre, but it's a long way from the main road, so it's not too noisy. It's also near the beach, and it has beautiful views across the bay.

Unit 9 Quantity

A A, some & any

1 some meat; some tomatoes; any cheese; a nice big piece; any spaghetti; a cheese sandwich
2 a bucket; some flour; some more; any elephants

B Quantity expressions

Possible answers:
1 There isn't much rain in the Sahara Desert.
2 Howard Hughes had a lot of money.
3 Not many countries have nuclear weapons.
4 Nurses don't earn much money.
5 A lot of people speak Spanish.
6 The Americans didn't find any gold on the moon.

C How much ...? & How many ...?

1 How many cigarettes does he smoke a day?
2 How much petrol is there in the car?
3 How much milk do you want?
4 How many people were there at the meeting?
5 How much (money) does she earn (a week)?
6 How many minutes are there in a day?
7 How much wine (How many bottles) did they buy?

D Too & enough

2 There aren't enough things to do in the evening.
3 There isn't enough fresh air.
4 There are too many burglaries.
5 There's too much rubbish in the streets.
6 There aren't enough public telephones.
7 There's too much noise from traffic.

Listening: Panel discussion

1 any good; too many; too few; news programmes; the right things
2 *a* 3   *b* –   *c* –   *d* 1   *e* 2
3 Wars and famines are important; the news often doesn't mention them.
   Some countries have a 24 hour news channel.
   People don't want to know about disasters.

Pronunciation: Secondary stress

2 *a* <u>Give</u> me a <u>**kiss**</u>.
   b <u>Let</u> me <u>**see**</u> it.
   c She <u>missed</u> her <u>**plane**</u>.
   d It's <u>time</u> to <u>go</u> to <u>**bed**</u>.
   e <u>How</u> many <u>**lang**</u>uages do you <u>speak</u>?
   f They <u>usually</u> have <u>lunch</u> at <u>**work**</u>.
   g <u>What</u> are you <u>doing</u> on <u>**Mon**</u>day?

Dictation

1 There isn't enough sport – I'd like to see more live matches.
2 I think there are too many quiz shows and chat shows. I'd like to see more serious programmes.
3 There are too many old black and white films. I'd like to see more modern films.
4 I think there are too many advertisements.
5 The news programmes aren't very good. They don't give enough international news.

Reading: Money

1	✔	✔	✔	✔	✔
2	✔	✘	✔	?	✔
3	✘	✔	?	✘	✔
4	✔	?	✔	✘	✘ (?)
5	✔	✔	✘	✔	✘

Unit 10 Clothes

A They come in pairs

1 shoes	4 shorts	7 tights
2 sandals	5 stockings	8 socks
3 trousers	6 jeans	9 earrings

B On and off

1 get undressed; take off 4 wear; get changed
2 got dressed; put on 5 took off; got undressed
3 tried ... on; wearing; took off

Listening: Working clothes

1 1: picture d; jeans, tracksuit, jacket, tie, shirt
  2: picture a; suit, skirt, blouse, trousers, jeans
  3: picture c; jeans, shorts, blouse, T-shirt, trousers, dress
  4: picture b; suit, shoes, pullover
2 1: works at home
  2: works for a solicitor
  3: a writer, works at home
  4: works in an office

Sound and spelling: Words with o (2)

2 D voice	D enjoy
C food	B wood
A before	A floor
A course	C loose
B look	C lose
C choose	B foot

3 Can you cook a good four course meal?
  If there's any more noise, I'll be annoyed.
  The boy was born at two in the morning.
  Look at the menu before you choose your food.

Dictation

A I like that denim jacket there. What do you think of it?
B Yes, it's nice. I love the colour. How much is it?
A £40.
B That's not too bad. Go on – try it on.
A Well, what do you think?
B I think it suits you, it's great. And it really goes with your trousers. What does it feel like?
A It's very comfortable. I think I'll buy it.

Writing skills: Sequence (1)

1 a then; after that; first
  b and then; and
2 Possible answer:
  First I collect the children from school. Then I take them to the park, and then we come home and we have supper together. After that I play with them for an hour, and then they have a bath and get ready for bed. Then I read them a story. After that I can sit down and relax.

Unit 11 Future plans

A New Year Resolutions: going to

Possible answers:
I'm going to smile.
I'm going to take the family out every weekend.
I'm going to visit my friends.
I'm not going to spend all my money on myself.
I'm going to buy lots of presents for the children.
I'm not going to get drunk.
I'm not going to watch TV all the time.
I'm going to have a bath and a shave every morning.

B Times and arrangements

Possible answers
The Browns are coming to dinner this evening.
He's going to the hairdresser's tomorrow morning.
He's attending his children's school concert tomorrow evening.
On Wednesday, he's having lunch with his in-laws.
He's giving a birthday party for his daughter on Friday.
Next week, his brother and family are coming to stay.
In two months, he's taking the family for a holiday at the seaside.

Listening: Two journeys

1 A ... Venice, Florence, Pisa, Rome, Venice ...
  B ... Paris, South of France, Barcelona ...
2 A (*ferry:* England–France)
    train: France–Venice
    car: Venice–Florence–Pisa–Rome–Venice
  B *ferry:* England–France
    train: coast–Paris (+ possibly Barcelona–London)
    hitch hike: Paris–South of France–Barcelona

Pronunciation: Rhythm

a **Go away**.
b There's a **fly** in my **soup**.
c They ar**rived** very **late**.
d **How** do you **do**?
e We're **meet**ing some **friends** for a **drink**.
f I **don't like cats**.
g **Are** you **rea**ding that **news**paper?

Dictation

1 I'm going to wear comfortable old clothes, and I'm not going to shave. I'm going to see my girlfriend, and I'm going to go to lots of parties. I'm going to eat lots of good home cooking.
2 I'm going to stay in bed every morning and read the newspaper. I'm not going to cook anything or wash anything. And I'm going to go out every single evening.

Reading: Letters

2 Valerie, Alan	6 Brigitte, Alan
3 Valerie	7 Valerie, Brigitte, Alan
4 Brigitte, Alan	8 Probably Alan
5 Valerie, Brigitte	

Unit 12 How do you feel?

A What's wrong

Diagram 1: 1 matter   2 ache   3 hurts   4 tired   5 rest
Diagram 2: 1▼ smoke   1▶ sick   2 chest   3 sore
4 teeth
Diagram 3: 1▶ how   1▼ happen   2 wrist   3 pain
4 better

B Good advice

Possible answers:
1 Read an English dictionary. Have a cup of hot chocolate.
2 Take an aspirin. Phone the dentist.
3 Don't eat so much. Go for a run.
4 Have something to drink. Stop smoking for a few days.

C Phrases

Possible answers:
1 make an appointment
2 you have toothache
3 examine your chest
4 take the pills
5 gave me a prescription
6 stay in bed
7 go to the chemist's

Listening: Feeling ill

1 *a* he was ~~at home~~ at work
  b he was ~~watching TV~~ working on his computer
  c he felt ~~cold~~ hot
  d his ~~throat~~ head hurt
  e examined his ears and ~~throat~~ eyes and chest
  f stay in bed for ~~a week~~ a few days
  g ~~only two~~ two or three days later he felt better
2 *a* He was tired from using his computer too much
  b He had a rest from using the computer

Sound and spelling: Words with *u*

2 D pull   D push
  A Sunday   B uniform
  A running   D sugar
  C curtains   C hurt
  B fruit   B include
  B student   A hungry
3 I usually go to church on Sunday.
  That jumper doesn't suit you.
  Does the supermarket sell fruit?
  Student nurses wear blue uniforms.

Dictation

Then he opened my mouth and looked at my tongue, and he felt my pulse, and he listened to my heart. Then he sat down and wrote a prescription. It said 'three good meals every day, one two-mile walk every morning, one bed at 11 o'clock every night, and don't read medical books!' I followed the doctor's instructions, and I am happy to say that I now feel quite well again.

Writing skills: Listing

2 *a* I really enjoyed the party. The food was delicious, there was lots of good music and I met some very interesting people.
  b I don't like my flat mate much. She never cleans the flat and she plays loud music all the time. Also, she has some very strange friends.
3 *Possible answers:*
  a There are long traffic jams and there's nowhere to park. Also it's terribly crowded everywhere.
  b It's just the right length, it's a very unusual colour, and it goes with your eyes.
  c His legs ached, his feet were sore and he felt tired and hungry.
  d It's very clean and the food's always freshly cooked. Also, the prices are quite reasonable.

Revision and extension Units 7–12

1 Verb forms

1 sent; didn't arrive
2 are coming; 're going
  (*or* are going to come; 're going to go)
3 drives; broke; isn't going (*or* 's not going)
4 sold; bought
5 was; weren't

2 Asking questions

1 Why did you leave your job?
  or Why did you give up your job?
2 How many states are there in the USA?
3 Have you got any money?
4 When did you arrive / get here / come?
5 Is there any butter?
  or Have you/we got any butter?
6 What would you like to drink?
  or What do you want to drink?
7 How much does it cost?
  or How much is it?

3 Prepositions

1 at the weekend
  on Wednesday
2 in about a month
3 to a new flat;
  in the suburbs
4 with my blue dress
5 on the 10th floor;
  of the river
6 on 16th March

4 Quantity expressions

1 too much television;
  too many parties;
  enough sleep (*or* any sleep)

2 any (*or* some) 10p pieces;
  some phone calls;
  How many;
  enough
3 a lot of (*or* enough) friends;
  enough money;
  any worries

5 Word order

1 He made an appointment to see the doctor.
2 We'll probably go out for a meal tonight.
3 She's wearing a pair of gold earrings.
4 He left home half an hour ago.
5 How much sugar is there in a kilo of jam?
6 The baby was born on Friday afternoon.

Unit 13 Comparison

A Comparative and superlative

smaller; smallest
fatter; fattest
wider; widest
heavier; heaviest
more careful; most careful
more exciting; most exciting
more intelligent; most intelligent
better; best
worse; worst
farther; farthest (*or* further; furthest)
more; most

B Opposites

1 Silver is *cheaper* than gold.
2 Sheep are *older* than lambs.
3 Aluminium is *lighter* than steel.
4 Arizona is *drier* than California.
5 Reading is *easier* than listening.
6 The West is *richer* than the Third World.
7 Mars is *colder* than Venus.

C World records

1 The USSR is the largest country in the world.
2 The whale is the largest mammal (animal) in the world.
3 The cheetah is the fastest animal (mammal) in the world.
4 The Nile is the longest river in the world.
5 M. Everest is the highest mountain in the world.
6 The Sahara is the sunniest place in the world.
7 Beluga is the best (most expensive) caviare in the world.

Listening: The most and the least

1 *a* A   *b* B   *c* B   *d* A   *e* A   *f* B
2 *a* None of them
  b Switzerland: B and C
    Mexico: B
    Japan: None of them

c Switzerland: A
  Mexico: A
  Japan: C

Pronunciation: Reduced vowels (3)

2 *a* 1 He doesn't speak to me any more.
  b 2 Careful! Those dogs are dangerous.
  c 1 Was the exam difficult?
  d 2 Where do you work?
  e 2 What does that word mean?
  f 2 You can sit wherever you like?
  g 1 Does she play chess? I think she does.
  h 2 His grandparents were Italian.
  i 2 I was there a few days ago.
  j 2 Are the children in bed?
  k 1 There weren't any seats left.
  l 2 How was the film? It was very good.

Dictation

1 London is Britain's largest city. Its most famous buildings are Buckingham Palace and the Houses of Parliament.
2 The greatest English writer, William Shakespeare, was born in Stratford-on-Avon in 1564. His most famous play is probably *Hamlet*.
3 The wettest place in Britain is the Lake District. It has about 440 cm (centimetres) of rain a year.
4 The River Severn is the longest river in Britain. It is 354 km (kilometres) long.

Reading: Four planets

1 T (It's 147 years)   7 F (Only 10 times bigger)
2 T   8 F (Pluto is)
3 T   9 T (Venus's is much thicker)
4 F (Venus is hotter) 10 T
5 T   11 T (It's the brightest)
6 T (Pluto's the lightest)

Unit 14 About town

A Guests

Possible answers:
1 take him to a nightclub; go to a casino
2 go sightseeing with her; take her to sit in the park; take her to a museum or an exhibition
3 take them to a football match; go to a sports centre; go swimming; take them to the cinema; take them to the zoo
4 go shopping with them; go sightseeing; go to a place with good views of the town; go to a nightclub or a disco(thèque)

B Giving directions

Possible answers:
1 Go under that bridge and then go straight on across the river, past the park, and turn left at the end of the road. You'll see the university on the left.

2 Yes. Go straight on down this road, and turn right at the church. The swimming pool's down there on the left.

3 – Excuse me, how do I get to the station?
– Take the first turning on the left, and then turn right at the supermarket. The station's at the end of the road.

C Describing towns

Possible answers:

1 There's a university, there are lots of cheap cafés and there's a good bookshop.

2 It's got some beautiful old buildings and it's by the sea.

3 There's nothing to do in the evenings, it's very small and it hasn't got a theatre.

4 There are lots of parks, it's got good schools, and there isn't too much traffic.

Listening: Living in London

1 *a* W; bad   *c* W; bad   *e* M; good
  b M; good   *d* W; bad   *f* M; good

2 *Possible answers:*
  b The theatre's 15 minutes from my home.
  c Aeroplanes go over every two minutes.
  d People are extremely rude.
  e You can buy fresh croissants.
  f It's very cosmopolitan.

Sound and spelling: Words with *y*

2 B dry   B typist
  A carry   A hungry
  A friendly   B trying

3 *a* married   *c* easier   *e* parties
  b cries   *d* enjoyed   *f* stays

4 Why are you typing so slowly?
  It's the friendliest city in the world.
  I'm trying to dry my hair.
  He gets angry very easily.

Dictation

Drive down Sunset Boulevard, probably the most famous street in Los Angeles. Here you can see every side of the city's character – cheap nightclubs side by side with smart boutiques and expensive restaurants. At the western end of the Boulevard is the Beverly Hills Hotel, where visiting film stars, directors and writers go to sign their contracts.

Writing skills: Reason and contrast

2 *a* Although   *b* As/Because   *c* but; so
  d so; but

3 *Possible answers:*
  a As it's a small town, it's easy to get to know people, and people are very friendly.
  b As there are factories all round the town the air's very polluted, so it's a very unhealthy place to live.
  c Although it's a large industrial town and it's quite

ugly, I like living there because it has a friendly atmosphere.

d Although it's only a small town, it's very lively and there's lots to do in the evenings, and as it's by the sea it's very popular with tourists.

Unit 15 Past and present

A Irregular squares

Top left: 1 ▶ left 1 ▼ lost 2 found 3 swum
Top right: 1 slept 2 flown 3 won 4 spent
Bottom left: 1 bought 2 sold 3 done 4 gone
Bottom right: 1 written 2 grown 3 woken
  4 taken 5 been

B Not ... yet

1 She hasn't found a flat yet.
2 They haven't come back yet.
3 He hasn't got up yet.
4 We haven't given up (smoking) yet.
5 The bus hasn't arrived yet.
6 I haven't left university yet.

D Questions of experience

Possible questions:

2 Have you ever driven a car?
3 Have you ever swallowed a fishbone?
4 Have you ever been to the Caribbean?
5 Have you ever spoken French in France?
6 Have you ever eaten Beluga caviare?
7 Have you ever acted in a play?
8 Have you ever been water skiing?

Listening: Have you ever ...?

1 1 ... been sailing?   4 ... seen a play by
  2 ... acted in a play?   Shakespeare?
  3 ... ridden a motorbike?   5 ... been to a casino?

2 1 has been sailing; on his ninth birthday; yes
  2 has acted in an opera; don't know; yes
  3 has ridden a motorbike; when she was 16; no
  4 has seen *Hamlet*; last week; yes
  5 hasn't been to a casino

3 *a* 3 – She went round the square four times.
  b 1 – He went sailing on his ninth birthday.
  c 2 – She was one of the people on stage.
  d 5 – You need lots of money to go into a casino.
  e 4 – She saw *Hamlet* at the Old Vic.

Pronunciation: Falling intonation

2 *a* I live in London.
  b We need more petrol.
  c Give it to me.
  d The matches are in the cupboard.
  e What are they doing?
  f We've just bought a new house.
  g They're watching television.

Dictation

Police are searching for four children who have been missing from their home near Glasgow for nearly 24 hours. The three five-year-old girls and a boy of three were last seen early yesterday afternoon by a neighbour. No-one has seen them since. Police have organised a search of the neighbourhood to try to find the four children.

Reading: Varieties of English

1 *a* 3   *b* 4   *c* 2   *d* 5   *e* 1   *f* 6
2 *a* No – he's still painting it (*text 3*)
  b No, it isn't (*text 5*)
  c Yes – he's leaving her (*text 6*)
  d Five – *Wildfire* and four others (*text 4*)
  e Teacher of business English (*text 2*)
  f David; yes (*text 1*)

Unit 16 Towns

A Two kinds of activity

1	guitar	7	jogging
2	knit	8	jump
3	dancing	9	football
4	cooking	10	riding
5	collects	11	golf
6	poetry	12	motor
		13	garden

A indoor   B outdoor

B Go, play and do

1 play; do   4 going; playing; went
2 do; goes   5 did; went; played
3 playing; played

Listening: Rock climbing

1 *a* ✔   *d* ✗
  b ✗   *e* ✔
  c ✔   *f* ✔
2 b
3 *Possible answer:*
  'Help! I'm going to break my arm.'
  'I'm definitely going to hurt myself.'

Sound and spelling: Words with *r*

2 D flower   E during
  B hear   B we're
  A they're   C fire
  E cure   A where
  D hour   B near
  A hair   C drier
3 Where's our hair drier?
  They're sitting near the fire.
  We're sending them some flowers to cheer them up.
  There's a shower upstairs in the bathroom.

Dictation

I'm very interested in languages, because when I go abroad I like to speak with the people there. I try to play the guitar – I don't play very well but every week I meet a friend and we both enjoy ourselves playing together. I live very near the sea. All through the year I go for walks along the shore, and in the summer I go swimming every day.

Writing skills: Sequence (2)

2 *a* I first met him at a party in London. About a year later I saw him again.
  b She put the phone down. After a few seconds, she picked it up again and dialled a number.
3 *Possible answers:*
  a and; A few minutes later; and
  b and; After half an hour
  c First; then; and; About an hour later
4 *Possible answer:*
  Monica knew exactly what to do. She wrote a letter and put it on the table. The letter said 'Goodbye, Edward. I've had enough.' Then she packed a small suitcase and called a taxi. After about ten minutes the taxi arrived. Monica closed the door and posted her keys through the letter box. Two hours later Edward arrived home.

Unit 17 Obligation

A Obligation structures

1 have to; can   5 don't have to; don't
2 mustn't   have to; can
3 must/have to; mustn't   6 Can; can; mustn't
4 must/have to

B Childish questions

Possible answers:
1 Do I have to go to the dentist's?
2 Can I have chips for lunch?
3 Do you have to go home now?
4 Can we stay up for a bit?
5 Do I have to go to school?

C Flying rules

Possible answers:
You mustn't smoke during take-off and landing, but you can smoke at other times. You can't smoke in the non-smoking seats or in the toilet.
You can take one piece of hand baggage. You have to put it under your seat or in the overhead lockers.
When the seat belt sign is lit, you have to stay in your seat. At other times, you can walk around the plane.
You don't have to take food and drink with you. They usually give you a meal during the flight.

D Giving advice

Possible answers:

2 ... you should take exercise and you shouldn't eat too much fatty food. You should eat a lot of fish, too.

3 ... you ought to wear a seat belt, and you ought not to drink any alcohol. You should also obey speed limits.

4 ... you should work hard, and you should pay your staff well. And you ought to be polite to your customers.

Listening: Radio phone-in

1 *a* who ~~has a job~~ is a student
  b a ~~bad~~ good relationship
  c he likes to ~~go to parties~~ stay at home
  d she prefers to ~~stay at home and read~~ go out
  e he won't ~~stay~~ go out with her
2 *a* 1   *e* 2
  b –   *f* –
  c 2   *g* –
  d 1

Pronunciation: Rising intonation

2 *a* Hello. ↘   *e* Do you drink coffee? ↗
  b Hello? ↗   *f* Where are you going? ↘
  c Are you busy? ↗   *g* He's a friend of mine. ↘
  d My name's Peter. ↘   *h* He's a friend of yours? ↗

Dictation

Last year, my girlfriend wanted to take a business course but she didn't have enough money. Now she's finished the course, and has found a good job, but she hasn't offered to pay me back. I've mentioned it once or twice, but she just laughs and talks about something else. I love my girlfriend, but I want my money back too.

Unit 18 A day's work

A Types of work

1 police	law
2 secretary	phone
3 actor	plays
4 nurse	patients
5 receptionist	deal
6 manager	money
7 porter	carry
8 writer	books
9 decorator	houses
10 student	read
11 assistant	customers
12 occupations	What do you do?

B Careers

1 applied; get
2 work; started (got); enjoying; leave
3 get
4 lost; looking (applying)
5 working
6 started; was; retires (leaves); get

Listening: A security guard

1 Securicor guards are hired by companies.
  Their job is to guard buildings.
  They prevent people from breaking into them.
2 *a* Yes   *d* No   *g* No
  b Yes   *e* Yes
  c No   *f* Yes

Sound and spelling: Hard and soft *c* and *g*

2 S ceiling   H figure
  S orange   H secret
  H copy   S agent
  H capital   S piece
  S fence   H apricot
  H magazine   S fridge
3 I think orange is an ugly colour.
  That magazine costs fifty cents a copy.
  The capital city is full of secret agents.
  There's a large dog behind the garden fence.

Dictation

1 I work in a hotel. I sit at the desk by the entrance. I deal with enquiries and reservations. Guests leave their keys with me when they go out.
2 I work for a large company. I have my own office and a secretary. I look after the company's money. Once a year I calculate the company's profits. It's a very well paid job.

Writing skills: Letter writing

2 *a* Elizabeth Burke
  b Don
  c Douglas Trafford
  d Miranda

Revision and extension Units 13–18

1 Sentences

1 don't have to
2 easiest language
3 more expensive than *or* dearer than
4 haven't found it
5 shouldn't eat *or* ought not to eat
6 've never *or* haven't
7 you mustn't

2 Asking questions

1 Who's taller, John or Richard?
2 Do I have to wear a suit?
3 Can/Could you tell me the way to the nearest bank?
4 Do you like/enjoy skiing ?
5 Have you ever played tennis?
6 Have they woken up yet? *or* Are they awake yet?
7 Are you still working for *Argos Travel*?

3 Prepositions

1 to a jazz concert
2 from her old job; for a new one
3 for my keys
4 at university
5 at the traffic lights; at the end; of the road
6 out of the window
7 into the net
8 for a package tour company; after the tourists; with any problems

4 Word order

1 They don't go to the theatre any more.
2 What time do you have to get to work?
3 She doesn't enjoy working as a tourist guide.
4 Go straight down this road and turn right.
5 Doctors earn more money than nurses.
6 I think Prague is the most beautiful city in Europe. *or* Prague is the most beautiful city in Europe, I think.

Unit 19 Narration

A What were they doing?

Possible answers:

2 ... were watching TV.
3 ... was having a bath.
4 ... was writing a letter.
5 ... were cooking dinner.
6 ... was getting dressed.
7 ... was having a shave.
8 ... was doing the ironing.
9 ... was playing cards.

B Short stories

Two possible answers:

1 My brother was practising the piano yesterday when he smelled smoke. He looked down and saw his cigarette lying on the carpet, so he picked it up quickly.
2 I was painting my bedroom ceiling the other day when I lost my balance and fell off the ladder. Luckily, I landed on the bed, so I wasn't hurt.

C ... -ing ... -ing ...

2 ... coming out of a hotel, carrying two suitcases.
3 ... sitting by the road, playing the saxophone.
4 ... wearing a helmet, digging a hole in the road.
5 ... standing by a piano, singing.
6 ... standing by a car, looking at the engine.
7 ... sitting in a café, drinking coffee.

Listening: Two stories

1 Story A: embarrassing, groom, reception, video, wallet
Story B: carriage, frightened, noise, platform, supporters, terrifying, underground
2 Story A: ... wedding ... video ... reception ... invited ... father ... groom ... wallet ... embarrassing.
Story B: ... an underground train ... football supporters
... noise ... carriage ... frightened ... doors ... tears

Pronunciation: Intonation: questions

2 *a* – Can you ski? ↗
– Yes I can. ↘
b – My car's broken down. ↘
– Oh, has it really? ↗
c – My name's Mifanwy. ↘
– Pardon? ↗
d – Did you see the film last night? ↗
– Yes, I did. ↘
– What did you think of it? ↘

Dictation

An old man with grey hair was sitting at the piano, playing a dance tune. In the centre of the room, in a space between the tables, a man and a woman were dancing cheek to cheek. There was a young couple holding hands in the corner, talking together in low voices. At another table, a group of six men were playing cards.

Reading: Bad luck

Superstition:

1 H	2 C or I	3 I or C	4 E	5 B
6 G	7 A	8 F	9 D	

The Thief:

1 C	2 G	3 F	4 H	5 B
6 D	7 A	8 E		

Unit 20 People

A Physical appearance

Possible answers:

She was in her 20s. She was quite tall and she had short fair hair. She was wearing a green dress and sunglasses. He was a bald man in his 70s, with a short grey beard and striking blue eyes. He was carrying a walking stick.

B Character adjectives

1 friendly	5 self-confident	9 lazy
2 mean	6 hard-working	10 generous
3 bad-tempered	7 honest	11 modest
4 shy	8 easy-going	12 selfish

Listening: Famous people

a Gandhi	g Gandhi
b Victoria	h Gandhi
c Napoleon	i Victoria
d Victoria	j Gandhi
e Napoleon	k Napoleon
f Victoria	l Napoleon

Sound and spelling: Long and short vowels

2 | | |
|---|---|
| L mute | S glutton |
| L coping | L scraper |
| S scram | S flitted |
| L pane | L inducing |
| L strive | S spottiest |
| S petty | L refinery |

3 They're having dinner in the dining room.
   He likes telling jokes.
   She's writing a letter to the newspaper.
   Are they winning the game or losing?

Dictation

1 It's a little stone cottage, it's grey stone, and it's very small, and there's some smoke coming out of the chimney.
2 Well, it needs a lot of work. Everything's neglected and overgrown. Very tall flowers, and very long grass.
3 It's a huge kind of lake, and the water's dark and calm, and there are fish in it. It's cold to swim in, but good too.

Writing skills: Relative clauses (1)

2 a I live in Stenton, which is a small village near Cambridge.
  b I've got three sisters, who are all older than me.
  c I've got a younger brother, who's in the army.
  d Pandas, which only eat bamboo, are becoming very rare.
3 a which was built in 70s
  b who are also staying in Paris
  c which is a kind of sausage
  d which is about 200 km south of here
  e who's studying art here
  f which still isn't very good

Unit 21 Prediction

B Questions with 'will'

1 What time (When …) will the train arrive?
2 Will it be windy tomorrow?
3 Will there be a general election this year?
4 Where will you be?
5 When will I see you again?
6 Will they lend us the money?
7 How much will the ticket cost me?

C If & unless

Possible answers:
1 If you wear a raincoat you won't get wet.
2 If you leave before dark, you'll get home safely.
3 Unless you apologise, I'll never speak to you again.
4 Unless you phone your parents, they'll worry about you.
5 Unless you go to bed early, you'll be tired tomorrow.
6 If you forget his birthday, he'll be very upset.
7 Unless you have a holiday, you'll be ill.

D Predictions with 'going to'

Possible answers:
1 It's going to rain.
2 She's going to have a baby.
3 I think I'm going to sneeze.
4 I think I'm going to be ill/sick.
5 It's going to crash (into the mountains).
6 You're going to fail. (*or* You're not going to pass.)
7 He's going to win (the race).
8 He's going to be all right.

Listening: Driving test

1 1 Which is your car?
  2 OK, off you go.
  3 Turn right at the crossroads.
  4 What did that road sign say?
  5 Stop!
  6 Park the car just here.
  7 Well, I'm glad to say you've passed your test.
2 a At a driving test centre.
  b Put you seat belt (safety belt) on.
  c A clipboard and some papers.
  d It means you've failed the test.

Pronunciation: Contrastive stress

2 a She was a **maths** teacher.
  b She **was** a maths teacher.
  c My **mot**her usually gets up early.
  d My mother **us**ually gets up early.
  e I didn't see him **yes**terday.
  f I didn't **see** him yesterday.

Dictation

1 Before you give blood they need to find out which blood group you belong to. So the nurse will take a small sample of blood from the end of your finger.
2 Just lie down and relax. The nurse will attach a needle to your arm, and the blood will flow down into a bag beside your bed. You don't have to do anything at all.

Reading: Star gazing

1 | | |
|---|---|
| a Sagittarius | f Taurus and Pisces |
| b Pisces | g Taurus |
| c Sagittarius and Libra | h Libra and Taurus |
| d Taurus | i Pisces and Taurus |
| e Libra and Sagittarius | j Pisces |

Unit 22 Around the world

A On the map

1 lake	5 border	9 desert
2 continent	6 forest	10 island
3 volcano	7 ocean	11 coast
4 river	8 mountain	12 environment

C International quiz

1 a Scotland   d Hungary
  b Thailand   e Ireland (Republic of)
  c Turkey   f Austria

2 a Brazilian   d South African
  b Portuguese e Polish (a Pole)
  c Canadian   f Danish (a Dane)

3 a Japanese   d Finnish
  b Italian   e Russian
  c French

4 a Spanish   d Arabic
  b Dutch   e Greek
  c German   f Chinese

Listening: Living in a hot climate

1 Yes
2 July and August
3 – (doesn't say)
4 No
5 – (doesn't say)
6 Yes
7 No (they're air-conditioned)
8 Yes (in air-conditioned buildings)
9 No (Not in summer)

Sound and spelling: Words with s

2 /s/ press   /z/ buys
  /z/ busy   /s/ scream
  /s/ coughs   /z/ climbs
  /s/ messy   /s/ listen
  /z/ princes   /z/ please
  /s/ princess   /z/ trousers
3 impress   essential
  disease   confused
  discloses   assumes
  distances   blossom

Dictation

The climate of Egypt is mainly hot and dry. Apart from the Valley of the River Nile, which runs through the country from south to north, it consists entirely of desert. In the summer, the temperature often reaches 45° in the south of the country, and 30° in the north. In winter, the weather is cooler, and along the north coast it is often cloudy, with occasional rain.

Writing skills: Relative clauses (2)

1 a Jakarta, which is the capital of Indonesia, has...
  b The Cape Verde Islands, which used to be a Portuguese colony, have been ...
  c ... of Charles I, who was King of England from 1600 to 1649
  d In Alaska, where the temperature often falls below –30°, it can be ... or In Alaska it can be dangerous to go out in winter, when the temperature ...

2 *Possible answer:*
  If you have time, you should visit the Parrot Café, which is in a small side street behind the harbour. It's the oldest café in the town and it's very popular with fishermen, who sit there all day playing cards. The owner, who is in his 80s, is a retired sea captain. Next to the Parrot Café there's a small museum, where you can see treasure from an old sailing ship, which sank near the town in the 17th century.

Unit 23 Duration

A For or since?

1 for; since	4 for; since; for
2 for; for	5 since; for
3 for; since	6 since; for; since; since

B Talking about duration

1 I've known him since my birthday party.
2 She's been asleep for a long time.
3 They've been learning Arabic since last autumn.
4 We've been divorced for six months.
5 I've been reading this book since yesterday lunchtime.
6 She's had her guitar since Christmas.
  (*or* She's been playing the guitar since Christmas.)
7 He's been wearing glasses for five years.

C How long ...?

1 How long have you known her?
2 How long have you had it?
3 How long have they been (staying) here?
4 How long has he been playing (the piano)?
5 How long has she been learning (speaking) it?
6 How long have you had it?
7 How long has she been there?

Listening: 24 hours

1 a 6 hours   e 3 hours
  b 2 hours   f 2 hours
  c 1½ hours   i 5 hours
  d 1 hour

2 a Housewife   d Evening meal
  b One   e Children's books
  c No   f Very tired

Pronunciation: Dialogues

A – I'm going to Spain next week. ↘
  – Are you? ↗ Who are you going with? ↘
  – Mary. ↘
  – Who? ↗
B – Would you like to come to the cinema tonight? ↗
  – No, I'm afraid I can't. ↘ I'm busy tonight. ↘
  – Are you free tomorrow, then? ↗
  – No, I'm busy tomorrow, too. ↘
C – Have you ever been to Malaysia? ↗
  – No I haven't, but I've been to Thailand. ↘
  – Oh. Were you there on holiday? ↗
  – No, not on holiday. ↘ It was a business trip. ↘

Dictation

1 I go to lectures from 9 till 12, and I have classes from 2 to 4. Apart from that I spend about 3 hours in the library or working in my room.
2 My flat's near the university. I don't spend more than half an hour a day travelling.
3 I don't eat breakfast, and I only have time for a quick lunch. Dinner's more relaxed. I suppose I spend about 2 hours altogether having meals.

Unit 24 But is it art?

A Places and people

play: theatre; playwright; actor; producer
opera: opera house; composer; orchestra/conductor; singer
symphony: concert hall; composer; orchestra; conductor
film: cinema; director; producer; actor
painting: art gallery; painter; exhibition

Listening: Choosing a painting

2 A ? Interesting for a few moments.
  B ? I'd find it rather disturbing.
  C ✗ I'd grow bored with it rather quickly.
  D ✔ It's a very warm painting.
  E ✔ A very peaceful painting.
  F ✔ Suitable for a hall.
3 E

Sound and spelling: Words with *th*

2 /θ/ earth   /θ/ thumb
  /ð/ theirs   /θ/ mouth
  /ð/ brother   /ð/ these
  /θ/ months   /ð/ neither
  /ð/ northern   /ð/ breathe
  /ð/ leather   /θ/ cloth
  /θ/ both   /ð/ clothes
3 I *think the* ship's sinking.
  Look – *there's another* mouse.
  Is the *clothes* shop open?
  Are *both those* seats taken?
  I taught for *three* years at a secondary school.
  Congratulations on the *birth* of your daughter.

Dictation

He reached the bed, took off his clothes and slid under the covers. He heard the soft breaths of the stranger and knew that he would never be able to get to sleep.
  'By the way,' he said hesitantly, after a while. 'My name is Schwamm.'
  'Uh-huh,' said the stranger.
  'Yes.'
  'Did you come here for a conference?'
  'No, and you?'
  'No.'
  'On business?' asked Schwamm.
  'Not really.'
  'I've probably got the most remarkable reason a man could have for travelling to this city,' said Schwamm.

Writing skills: Sequence (3)

2 *a* A few weeks after he bought...
    or A few weeks after buying...
  b Two years later, she had...
  c Before leaving the house...
    or Before I left the house...
  d Two years after joining...
    or Two years after he joined...
  e While staying in India, she...
3 *Possible answer:*
  After she said goodbye to her friends, she went back to the hotel. Fortunately, there was no one at the desk, so she quickly took the key for Room 24 and took the lift to the second floor. Before opening the door she put her ear to the keyhole and listened carefully. Then she slipped quietly into the room and switched the light on. A few minutes later, she found what she was looking for. The book was in the wardrobe under some shirts. She looked quickly through it, and then, after putting the book back in the wardrobe, she left the room.

Revision and extension Units 19–24

1 Verb forms

1 spent; playing
2 was standing; came; pushed
3 's been playing; 'll win
4 leave; 'll call
5 sitting; playing; was singing
6 'm going to be

2 Asking questions

1 How much (money) will they pay (me)? or How much (money) will I get/earn?
2 How long have you had that jacket?
3 What does he look like?
4 What were you talking about?
5 What's the climate/weather like in Malaysia?
6 How long have you been giving/going to/taking/having private lessons?
7 What do you think of that picture?

3 Prepositions

1 along the road;
  at the bus stop
2 in her fifties
3 at the airport;
  through customs
4 on the coast;
  in the mountains
5 for nearly an hour;
  since 9 o'clock this morning
6 from 8 in the morning;
  to/till/until 6 in the evening;
  to an evening class
7 of the woman's face;
  by Picasso

4 Word order

1 The telegram arrived while they were having lunch.
  or
  While they were having lunch, the telegram arrived.
2 She's a tall woman with long dark hair.
3 How long will it take to get home?
4 Her brother is about 25 years old.
5 The best time to visit Scotland is the early summer.
  or
  The early summer is the best time to visit Scotland.
6 If you don't hurry you might not get a ticket. *or*
  You might not get a ticket if you don't hurry.

Irregular verbs

Infinitive	Simple past	Past participle
be	was/were	been
become	became	become
begin	began	begun
blow	blew	blown
break	broke	broken
bring	brought	brought
build	built	built
buy	bought	bought
can	could	(been able)
catch	caught	caught
choose	chose	chosen
come	came	come
cost	cost	cost
cut	cut	cut
do	did	done
draw	drew	drawn
dream	dreamt	dreamt
drink	drank	drunk
drive	drove	driven
eat	ate	eaten
fall	fell	fallen
feed	fed	fed
feel	felt	felt
find	found	found
fly	flew	flown
forget	forgot	forgotten
get	got	got
give	gave	given
go	went	gone (been)
have	had	had
hear	heard	heard
hide	hid	hidden
hit	hit	hit
hold	held	held
hurt	hurt	hurt
keep	kept	kept
know	knew	known
lay	laid	laid
learn	learnt	learnt
leave	left	left
lend	lent	lent
let	let	let
lie	lay	lain
lose	lost	lost
make	made	made
mean	meant	meant
meet	met	met
pay	paid	paid
put	put	put
read	read	read
ride	rode	ridden
ring	rang	rung
rise	rose	risen
run	ran	run
say	said	said
see	saw	seen
sell	sold	sold
send	sent	sent
set	set	set
shake	shook	shaken
shine	shone	shone
shoot	shot	shot

Infinitive	Simple past	Past participle
show	showed	shown
shut	shut	shut
sing	sang	sung
sit	sat	sat
sleep	slept	slept
speak	spoke	spoken
spell	spelt	spelt
spend	spent	spent
stand	stood	stood
steal	stole	stolen
swim	swam	swum
take	took	taken
teach	taught	taught
tear	tore	torn
tell	told	told
think	thought	thought
throw	threw	thrown
understand	understood	understood
wake	woke	woken
wear	wore	worn
win	won	won
write	wrote	written

Phonetic symbols

Vowels

Symbol	Example
/iː/	tree /triː/
/i/	many /ˈmeni/
/ɪ/	sit /sɪt/
/e/	bed /bed/
/æ/	back /bæk/
/ʌ/	sun /sʌn/
/ɑː/	car /kɑː/
/ɒ/	hot /hɒt/
/ɔː/	horse /hɔːs/
/ʊ/	full /fʊl/
/uː/	moon /muːn/
/ɜː/	girl /gɜːl/
/ə/	arrive /əˈraɪv/
	water /ˈwɔːtə/
/eɪ/	late /leɪt/
/aɪ/	time /taɪm/
/ɔɪ/	boy /bɔɪ/
/əʊ/	home /həʊm/
/aʊ/	out /aʊt/
/ɪə/	hear /hɪə/
/eə/	there /ðeə/
/ʊə/	pure /pjʊə/

Consonants

Symbol	Example
/p/	pull /pʊl/
/b/	bad /bæd/
/t/	take /teɪk/
/d/	dog /dɒg/
/k/	cat /kæt/
/g/	go /gəʊ/
/tʃ/	church /tʃɜːtʃ/
/dʒ/	age /eɪdʒ/
/f/	for /fɔː/
/v/	love /lʌv/
/θ/	thick /θɪk/
/ð/	this /ðɪs/
/s/	sit /sɪt/
/z/	zoo /zuː/
/ʃ/	shop /ʃɒp/
/ʒ/	leisure /ˈleʒə/
/h/	house /haʊs/
/m/	make /meɪk/
/n/	name /neɪm/
/ŋ/	bring /brɪŋ/
/l/	look /lʊk/
/r/	road /rəʊd/
/j/	young /jʌŋ/
/w/	wear /weə/

Stress

We show stress by a mark (ˈ) before the stressed syllable:
later /ˈleɪtə/; arrive /əˈraɪv/; information /ˌɪnfəˈmeɪʃn/

Acknowledgements

The authors and publishers would like to thank the following institutions and teachers for their help in testing the material and for the invaluable feedback which they provided.

ILI, Heliopolis, Egypt; The British Council, Cairo, Egypt; Lille University, Lille, France; IFG Langues, Paris, France; British Intstitute in Paris, Paris, France; IFERP, Paris, France; Beatrice Schildknecht, Wedel/Holstein, Germany; Heather Weyh, KONE, Hannover, Germany; The British Council, Athens, Greece; ELTE Radnóti Miklós Gyakorló Iskola, Budapest, Hungary; International House, Budapest, Hungary; Associazione Culturale delle Lingue Europee, Bologna, Italy; Teach In Language and Training Workshop, Rome, Italy; Cambridge Centre of English, Modena, Italy; British Institute of Florence, Florence, Italy; Toyohashi University of Technology, Toyohashi, Aichi-Ken, Japan; Cambridge School, Granollers, Spain; Senior Citizen Language and Cultural Centre, Zurich, Switzerland; Klubschule, Lichtensteig, Switzerland; Marmara Üniversitesi, Istanbul, Turkey; Yapi ve Kredi Bankasi, A.S., Istanbul, Turkey; Eyüboğlu Lisesi, Istanbul, Turkey; Ortadoğu Ingilizce Kurslari, Ankara, Turkey; London Study Centre, London, UK; Davies's School of English, London, UK; Eurocentre, Cambridge, UK; Studio School of English, Cambridge, UK; Newcastle College of Further Education, Newcastle, UK; Anglo World, Oxford, UK; International House, London, UK; Godmer House School of English, Oxford, UK; Chichester School of English, Chichester, UK.

The authors and publishers are grateful to the following copyright owners for permission to reproduce copyright material. Every endeavour has been made to contact copyright owners and apologies are expressed for any omissions.

p. 21: Illustrations and adapted text from the *Longman Illustrated Animal Encyclopedia*, edited by Dr Philip Whitfield, published 1984. Reprinted by kind permission of Longman Group UK.
p. 65: Reproduced and adapted from *The Usborne Book of Space Facts* by permission of Usborne Publishing Ltd, London.

The authors and publishers are grateful to the following illustrators:

Rowan Barnes-Murphy: pp. 41, 43, 59, 65, 76, 97, 107;
Helena Greene: pp. 13, 32;
Lisa Hall: pp. 11*t*, 69;
Jeremy Long: pp. 11*b*, 12, 39, 44, 66;
Michael Ogden: pp. 30, 48;
Bill Piggins: pp. 17, 18, 36, 50, 51, 56, 63, 74, 81, 82, 108;
Sue Shields: p. 93;
Tess Stone: pp. 20, 99;
Kathy Ward: p. 94;
Annabel Wright: pp. 23, 24, 28, 29, 47, 70, 92;
Clare Wyatt: pp. 52, 88, 91.

t = top   *b* = bottom